Experience

Research

Social Change

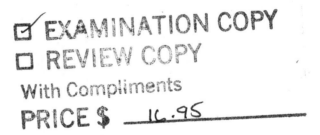

Experience

Research

Social Change

Methods from the Margins

Sandra L. Kirby
Department of Sociology
University of New Brunswick

Kate McKenna

Garamond Press

A publication of Garamond Press

Garamond Press
67A Portland Street
Toronto, Ontario M5V 2M9

Cover design: Peter McArthur
Typesetting: Coach House Press

Printed and bound in Canada

Canadian Cataloguing in Publication Data

Kirby, Sandra L. (Sandra Louise)
    Experience research social change

Bibliography: p.
Includes index.
ISBN 0-920059-82-1

1. Research — Methodology.   I. McKenna, Kate.
II. Title.

Q180.55.M4K5 1989   001.4'2   C89-094303-6

Acknowledgements

This book would not have been possible without the inspiration, contributions, enthusiasm and support we received from many people throughout the process. We are especially indebted to:

... the intellectual work of the many people we refer to throughout the book, which has inspired and influenced our thinking. In particular, we want to acknowledge our indebtedness to bell hooks, Audre Lorde and Dorothy Smith. Their work stresses the need to incorporate the actual experiences of people on the margins within any theory, method and practice for social change.

... all the women in the feminist methodology courses who helped us to develop our understanding of research from the margins and who so generously allowed us to use their research projects as examples.

... the many women with whom we have collaborated over the years on many political and intellectual projects, for their friendship, inspiration and wisdom.

Many people have helped during the various stages of preparation. We would particularly like to thank Amanda LeRougetel for providing precise and kindly editorial guidance, careful reading, invaluable suggestions and ongoing support throughout the writing of the book; and Errol Sharpe in particular and the people at Garamond Press in general (Sharon Nelson, Peter Saunders and Peter McArthur) for enthusiastically supporting the project.

Kate would particularly like to thank Neil Purcell. His loving support, intellectual companionship, patience and encouragement nurtured and sustained her throughout the writing of this book.

Sandi would like to mark the contributions of Amanda, Stevie and

Bounty to this work. Their views have shaped and clarified her understanding of the issues in research from the margins and the interdependence of community activism, academe and love of life.

We have benefited greatly from the generosity of friends and colleagues during the course of writing this book. It is a pleasure to thank them for their help.

S.K. and K.M.
March 1989

Foreword

This book is about doing your own research. You can use this book as a "How To Research" guide: starting from your experience and your interest in finding more information about the things that concern you, you can be a researcher. It differs from other research guides in that the methods described are based on the belief that we must include our own experience and understanding as part of doing research. This means that we must invest part of ourselves in the process of creating new information. We are an ingredient of our own research.

To make best use of this book, we suggest that you think of yourself as an active seeker of information about something that concerns you, an issue that has occupied your thoughts or a need that you have been aware of for some time. This book will be equally useful if you are part of a group that wants to do its own research. In either case, as a producer of new information you will learn as much about yourself as you do of the experience of others.

In the introduction, you will find the keys to help you read the book and answers to questions such as "What is research?" "What is the margin?" and "How can I do my own research?" Note the special meanings of the following terms as we use them. The **margins** refers to the context in which those who suffer injustice, inequality and exploitation live their lives. People find themselves on the margins not only in terms of resources. Knowledge production is also organized so that the views of a small group of people are presented as objective, as "The Truth." The majority of people are excluded from participating as either producers or participants in the creation of knowledge.

Research means gathering and making sense of information and acting responsibly with that information. **Method** means the way in which we gather the information and analyze it. There are many different methods and, in this book, we explore those which can meet our needs for researching from the margins. These terms and others are defined more fully in the Glossary at the end of the Introduction. They are to alert you to our particular way of using certain words and also to provide you with a ready reference for the language until it becomes second nature to you.

You will also find a schematic diagram of researching from the margins. We know that it is difficult to experience a new process step by step without clearly knowing what awaits you at the other end. The schematic diagram can be used as an ongoing reference so that you can understand each step you take in relation to the steps before and the steps that follow.

At the end of the book, we have included a list of researchers whose work is referred to throughout the book. Their research projects have benefited from, and contributed to, the development of the methodology presented here. There is also an index — a sort of back door key to lead you quickly to such terms as research question, conceptual baggage, analysis, filing, ethics and action. The index can also be used as a shortcut to find the page with just the graphic and just the description that you need to use in your own research description.

Other features of this book include an introduction which discusses who we are, why we wrote the book, how it was written and its social context; a chapter of short tasks you can do to get some data gathering practice; a chapter answering the question "What do we do with our research now that it's done?" and an annotated bibliography of references for further work.

Contents

A. PART ONE: 13

INTRODUCTION   15
GLOSSARY OF TERMS   31
SCHEMA   37

B. PART TWO: DOING RESEARCH   39

CHAPTER 1: GETTING READY   41
INTRODUCTION   41
WHAT IS RESEARCH?   43
BEGINNING THE PROCESS   44
1. Identifying your research interest   44
2. Framing your question   47
3. Conceptual baggage: how to do it   49
SUMMARY AND CHECKPOINTS   53

CHAPTER 2: GETTING FOCUSSED   54
INTRODUCTION   54
GETTING FOCUSSED   54
1. Freeing up our thinking: library tour   54
2. Refocussing on the question: finding just the right question   60
SUMMARY   61

CHAPTER 3: GEARING UP FOR DATA GATHERING   63
INTRODUCTION   63
OVERVIEW OF THE METHODS:
LOOKING AT THE OPTIONS FOR DATA GATHERING   64
1. Method One – Interviews   66
2. Method Two – Surveys   74
3. Method Three – Participant observation   76
4. Method Four – Life histories   81
5. Method Five – Unobtrusive measures   84
6. Summary   85
PRACTICING / LEARNING RESEARCH SKILLS   85
Five practice tasks   85
15 minute interview   86
A sample survey   88
Observation on site   89
Life history   91
Unobtrusive recording   92
SUMMARY AND CHECKPOINTS   93

CHAPTER 4: PLANNING FOR DATA GATHERING   95
INTRODUCTION
PLANNING THE RESEARCH   95
1. We are all creators of knowledge   95
2. Knowledge exists in many places   96
3. Who has the information?   97
4. Where do I have to go to get the information?   102
PLANNING THE DATA GATHERING   103
SETTING THE STAGE   106
SUMMARY AND CHECKPOINTS   110

CHAPTER 5: GATHERING DATA   111
INTRODUCTION   111
DATA GATHERING   111
1. Making contacts   111
a. Contact with potential participants and documentary discourse   114
b. Contact to gain access to settings   118
2. Beginning to gather data   119
3. Collecting and recording the data   124
4. Reflecting on the data   125
SUMMARY AND CHECKPOINTS   126

CHAPTER 6: PREPARING FOR ANALYSIS AND ANALYSIS 128
INTRODUCTION 128
ORGANIZING THE DATA 130
1. Managing the data 130
2. Expanding the files 131
a. Identity file 131
b. Tape file 132
c. Document file 133
d. Content file 133
e. Process file 133
3. Preparing for analysis 134
UNDERSTANDING THE DATA 138
1. Analyzing the data 138
a. Analysis files: content 138
b. Analysis files: process 144
c. Analysis within data categories 145
d. Analysis between data categories 146
2. Living with the data and revising the analysis 150
SUMMARY AND CHECKPOINTS 154

CHAPTER 7: PRESENTING THE ANALYSIS 155
INTRODUCTION 155
PRESENTING THE ANALYSIS 155
1. Writing a draft 156
2. Tips on writing 158
3. Voices in context 161
4. Sharing analysis with the research participants 163
5. Editing for the final report 163
ACTING ON WHAT WE KNOW 164
1. Getting the word out 164
2. Moving from research to action 165
SUMMARY AND CHECKPOINTS 167

CONCLUSION 169
BIBLIOGRAPHY 171
APPENDICES
Appendix A: DESCRIPTION OF RESEARCH PROJECTS 175
Appendix B: ANNOTATED BIBLIOGRAPHY 178
INDEX 182

Part One

Introduction

Women have often felt insane when cleaving to the truth of our experience. Our future depends on the sanity of each of us, and we have a profound stake, beyond the personal, in the project of describing our reality as candidly and fully as we can to each other. (Rich, 1979:190)

We live in a world in which knowledge is used to maintain oppressive relations. Information is interpreted and organized in such a way that the views of a small group of people are presented as objective knowledge, as "The Truth." We believe that Maria Mies is right when she says that "Research, which so far has been largely the instrument of dominance and legitimation of power elites, must be brought to serve the interests of dominated, exploited and oppressed groups" (1983:123). It is our hope that the content and process we describe in this book will contribute to this effort.

People have begun to challenge the way language, research and knowledge are used as instruments of power that impose form and order for the purpose of control. Whether it be calls from the governments of third world countries demanding what they have called a New World Information Order,[1] progressive literacy workers and popular educators using the context of learning as a means of transforming social relations, or feminists challenging the way knowledge is produced and whose view of the world it represents, they are all questioning **the monopoly that certain powerful groups hold over information**.

---

1. For more information on the New World Information Order see *The Politics Of Information*, CBC-Radio Ideas, May 1983.

Because many people cannot read or write they do not have access to information that could affect the quality of their daily lives, and in some instances their actual survival. Many literacy workers have pointed to the connection between cultural domination and illiteracy.

Most of us have not had the opportunity to research, to create knowledge which is rooted in and representative of our experience. We have been excluded from participating in, describing and analyzing our own understanding of reality.

If we think of research as a form of literacy, some of the insights which have grown out of progressive literacy work become helpful in understanding research from the margins. Progressive literacy workers stress that "the only valid form of literacy training is one which enables the learner to intervene in reality;" literacy education "must serve the purpose of teaching people how to demythologize and decode their culture" (Bee, 1980:50). Without analysis of the social context, the workers argue, literacy remains merely functional, enabling people to function within the status quo rather than allowing them to interact with and change society (Bee, 1980; Darville, forthcoming). And so it is with research; research that does not reflect on and analyze the social context from which it springs serves only the status quo and does not enable us to interact with and change society.

Reading and writing are skills that are context dependent. Many of us have at times found ourselves feeling either hesitation, frustration, insecurity or anger as we have tried to understand written information. Our hesitation involves more than simple lack of skill. It occurs "when [we] encounter an unfamiliar form of literacy, and the skills [we] do have seem 'out of place'" (Darville, forthcoming).

One of the major themes in discussions of literacy is the assertion that literacy has more than one form, that no single definition is sufficient since "literacy is more than a mechanical set of skills ... practices of reading and writing are bound within specific uses by particular actors from their different positions in the social order" (Weinstein, 1984:480). What this means is that whether people are literate or illiterate depends on the specific context in which they find themselves. Literacy can only be determined with reference to particular needs and uses for those skills which themselves vary and change over time and place.

We would argue that research needs are also context dependent. Although some people have claimed that research is capable of representing everyone equally because it is done in an objective, non-involved manner, women and people from various oppressed groups have been challenging such positivist (see Glossary) claims. They say that in fact research has not been objective and that it does not represent their experience. Rather, they argue, research and knowledge are produced in a manner which represents the political and social interests of a particular group. They point out that research has often been a tool of domination which has helped perpetuate and maintain current power relations of inequality. Too often the experts who do research have been well trained in patterns of thinking which not only conflict with their understanding, but explain and justify a world many are actually interested in changing.

It is important that the process of investigating the world not remain a specialized activity. Our everyday lives teach us skills which we use to observe and reflect on our experience. We focus on problems, ask questions, collect information and analyze and interpret "data." We already "do research" as we interact with the everyday world.

When we talk about doing research from the margins we are talking about being on the margins of the production of knowledge. In researching from the margins we are concerned with how research skills can enable people to create knowledge that will describe, explain and help change the world in which they live.

> We need to reclaim, name and re-name our experience and thus our knowledge of this social world we live in and daily help to construct, because only by doing so will it become truly ours, ours to use and do with as we will. (Stanley and Wise, 1983:205)

Think of the way in which graffiti is sometimes used as social comment, a sort of advertising from the margins, for example:

> If voting could change the system it would be illegal
> Too many causes without a rebel
> Get your ads off my body
> We're poor and we know why

These comments are made by individuals who are "making sense of" or ana-lysing their experience **from the margins**. These people are not only making sense but taking action by claiming public space to express their analysis, space normally monopolized by mainstream comment.

Researching from the margins shares some characteristics with advertis-ing from the margins in that:

- it can be done without a great deal of money;
- it can be collaborative and creative;
- it carries an alternative viewpoint;
- it can highlight the ways in which information is controlled;

- it can turn the language of the status quo back on itself;
- it often uses rage and humour to critique the status quo;
- it most often is not institutionalized.

We seek to describe a way of researching that incorporates an understanding of living in an antagonistic world and the need to act on such knowledge. Through research, we can begin to take control of the information we present and that which is presented on our behalf.

WHO ARE WE?
Kate:

Returning to university as a mature student in the summer of 1986, I became very aware of the real limitations of the form, language and subject matter which are required from a student / academic in order to be taken seriously. I understood that I was being trained / socialized to communicate with / in the terms of the dominant institutions. Personal experience was dismissed. As Richard Darville has so clearly said, in the dominant literacy, which is organizational, "what counts is how matters can be *written up* (to enter them into the organizational process), not how they can be *written down* (as an aid to memory or a way of relating experience)" (forthcoming).

During this same time I had a conversation with a friend who works in a shelter for battered women. She asked me if I could recommend written resources she could pass on to the women she works with. She said she often feels resourceless since so much of what is written is in a language that is difficult to read or understand. Although I had been focussing on writings about violence against women, I could think of nothing to suggest. This made me question just who academic work is being done for.

My interest in a practical guide to doing research comes partly from my experience as an activist in grassroots community groups. I began to notice how often we seemed to be doing the same things over and over without making significant change. It became clear that while individuals and groups learned a great deal as they organized to bring about change, much of that knowledge remained unrecorded.

This seems to have both positive and negative consequences. Although there may be a real sense of excitement as people discover what appear to be unexplored territories, my own experience suggests that the demands of what is perceived as a solitary journey soon take their toll. Often this means that both practical and theoretical knowledge is lost when people leave a group, or the group disbands.

It seems to me that most often the people who do get to record, reflect and learn from our experience are closely associated with what Dorothy Smith has called the "main business" or "the ruling apparatus" (1984). The managers of the state and business bureaucracies are examining, organizing and acting on their knowledge of the world all the time. Part of what it means to be outside the "ruling apparatus" is that we don't hear our own stories. If our experience is described, it is usually explained in terms and language that are not our own. When we begin to interpret ourselves and say together with others on the margins that "this is my story, this is our story," the power dynamics begin to shift.

Sandi:

The kind of people we are is at the root of what, how and why we research. We bring our Self as a resource to our researching. Look at how differently the following researchers would begin to look at athlete retirement: an athlete going through the experience, a sport sociologist, a feminist, an athlete's rights advocate and a popular journalist.

I am a teacher, educator, activist, athlete and researcher. The excitement I have experienced both as a researcher creating knowledge and as a teacher sharing that knowledge is the impetus for my involvement in writing this book.

I did not begin the research journey as a teacher but as a student. As I travelled along I tried unsuccessfully to be objective about things that I cared passionately about. I learned early on that who I am circumscribes what kind of research I can do.

My own understanding of doing practical research began when, as a master's student at McGill University in the 1970's, I did a quantitative study on preferred leadership styles among athletes of the novice and high-performance levels (Kirby, 1980). I tried mightily to distance myself, to be objective, to be removed from the research as it developed and to present the consequences of the study as if they all mattered equally. But, as a high performance athlete at the time, my biography was thoroughly intertwined with the research project. I cared about how it would turn out and what it might change. Although the study was partly a replication of some earlier work, the thrill of finding out something unknown began to grow in me. I learned then that my research Self and my athlete Self were at the centre of the whole research process.

In 1981, I did a nationwide survey on the gender inequities in the sport of rowing (Kirby, 1981). It was exciting work because it was action-oriented, that is, people were waiting for the information and were going to act on the recommendations from the study. It was a chance to begin to improve the quality of the sport experience for females and males alike. I was still an elite athlete at the time and I had a vested interest in the results. It did not occur to me that I knew too much to do a good job of researching. I simply used the methods available for sound survey research and proceeded to gather the much needed information. I am convinced that the product of that research is the richer because of my own experiences and my closeness to others within sport.

Routine research never appealed to me. By 1984, I was gathering information about how female athletes retired from high-performance sport. The research question and the method emerged from comparisons between what I had personally experienced in retiring and what I found in the available research. The gap astounded me. When I didn't find my experience represented in the research, I began to ask "have I retired wrong?" However, with time and a developing consciousness, I determined instead that the researchers had not paid particular attention to the experiences of women. From that point on, I knew that my Self was absolutely necessary and integral to the research and should not be discounted from it.

I was once told by a learned colleague that I was mistaken if I thought I knew something about sport. The message was that the theoretical examination of sport took precedence over my experience as an Olympic athlete who had lived and worked (and continues to live and work) in the sport culture. I remember being alternately cowed and furious. I recognize now that theoretical examination must be strongly rooted in the very experience it claims to explain.

As I was developing my doctoral research, Judith Golec[2] allowed me room to develop a method for researching that incorporated both my participant experience and my feminism. I had so many questions. Among them:

- How can I account for what I know?
- How am I to frame a question?
- How can I make the research I do in academia relevant to me and to other athletes?
- How much of the process is negotiable?
- How much of the fathers of sociology do I have to master just to do this research?
- How much of the research will be useful to the athletes who still have the experience ahead of them?
- Will what I find advance the understanding of women and sport?

It was Judith who introduced me to Glaser and Strauss, *The Discovery of Grounded Theory* (1967), and to one of the ways of accounting for

---

2. Dr. Judith Golec, Department of Sociology, University of Alberta, Edmonton, Alberta, Canada.

personal experience and preliminary understandings, the self-interview.[3] The information that comes out of this self-interview is what Judith calls **conceptual baggage**: it is information about the researcher that places her/him in relation to the research question and research process in an immediate and central way. By doing conceptual baggage, not only at the beginning of the whole research enterprise but in an ongoing way throughout the research, researchers enable their personal experiences, thoughts and feelings to enter into the research information on the same level as those of subsequent participants.

Throughout my Ph.D. research, I never lost the longing to have athletes' voices speaking about their experiences come through in the writing of my dissertation. After surveys and interviews were complete, I remember working through each bit of information until I could clearly hear the voices of the women in their accounts. It was only then that I "had it right" and was able to think about writing a final report. Even now, that sense of intimacy remains and that living, breathing data remains ever so.

Now I am teaching university methods courses. I have spent the past three years in classes of between five and ten women, all intent on learning by doing research that is meaningful and **honourable.** What has developed is a way of creating knowledge that adheres to principles of women's movement activism and academic rigour. Among these principles are the essentialness of accounting for the experience of the researcher in the research, of giving priority to the voices of the participants, of an egalitarian research process and of contextualizing the research.

WHY ARE WE WRITING THE BOOK?
1. We found an obvious "how-to" gap that needed to be filled.

During the past two years, as we have been teaching, developing and / or using this research method, we have found that questions about research spring up everywhere. As we talked about our work we discovered that other people were struggling with similar research questions and needs. They too were critical of mainstream research both because it is based on assumptions which often support and legitimate particular political and social interests,

---

3. The self-interview is one way of recording what the researcher already knows and thinks about a research topic. It is best if the researcher invites another person to the self-interview to facilitate the researcher's exploration during the tape recording of the interview. We suggest that the researcher prepare questions or themes which can be referred to in the interview. The facilitator can interject with comments or other questions. After the interview, the tape recording is transcribed and becomes part of the field notes.

and also because it ignores many areas of experience. Over and over again they would identify the need to connect this critical understanding of mainstream research with "how-to" skills that would enable them to begin to "do research differently." We came to realize that the research process that we were using was not widely known.

> Neil was trying to find a way to "stand in the shoes" of children he would soon be teaching who had hearing disabilities. Through his research, Neil hoped to get a better understanding of an experience he didn't have. He knew that the quantitative methods which he was being steered towards would not allow him to get close to aspects of the experience he intuitively knew were important. Even when he finally found an advisor who supported his qualitative research project, a week long simulation of hearing loss, he encountered a real poverty of information about how to analyze the information he had gathered.

> Errol had gathered quantities of data, including the diaries of three generations of women in a family in rural Prince Edward Island. As he talked with advisors about how he could go about his analysis, he found himself being directed toward a political economy framework. He knew from his own rural PEI roots that much of the rich experiential knowledge would be lost with such an analysis. Yet he found little support and few resources to help him "get at" the information he knew was important.

2. There is a need to move beyond the traditional academic understanding that knowledge can be created in a vacuum, and begin to claim and incorporate the personal and political context from which the knowledge springs as part of the data gathering process.

Becky, a graduate theology student, told us:

> In my classes we have been critiquing research that claims to have been done in an objective fashion. Women and people from various minority groups are saying that it's not objective, that it's coming from a particular group who have specific political and social interests.... I want to research something I'm really interested in and that does have a stake in my life and other people's lives. I want to know how research can be done differently, but I'm not sure what that means.

3. We believe research must begin to reflect the experience and concerns of people who have traditionally been marginalized by the research process and by what gets counted as knowledge.

It is impossible to discuss research without talking about power and influence. Differences in wealth and power separate people into identifiable groups, separate the "haves" from the "have nots": the rich from the poor; men from women; white people from people of colour; the overdeveloped countries of the world from the exploited countries. The list is endless.

We have all heard the expression "knowledge is power." One of the basic elements of power is that those who have positions of power are able to manufacture ideas. Another is being able to place ideas that have been created into the public agenda. Edward Bernays, a spokesperson for the public relations industry and the recipient of academic honours for his contributions to applied psychology, introduced the term "engineering of consent." The term describes the "freedom to persuade and suggest" which he characterizes as "the very essence of the democratic process." In a democracy, consent is not often achieved through force, but through the "domination of the flow of information and the means for expressing opinion or analysis" (Chomsky, 1981:140).

Because research is done by particular people in specific social and historical contexts, these have implications which need to be acknowledged.

> All knowledge that is about human society, and not about the natural world, is historical knowledge, and therefore rests upon judgement and interpretation. That is not to say that facts and data are nonexistent, but that facts and data get their importance from what is made of them in interpretation. (Said, 1981:154-56)

The act of interpretation underlies the entire research process. The act of interpretation is not something which occurs only at one specific point in the research after the data has been gathered; rather, interpretation exists at the beginning and continues throughout the entire process. What kind of data and facts you are able to gather will depend on the kind of questions you think are important to ask and the way in which you go about asking them. The research process is a social activity which is located in a specific historical and social context, and involves intentional activity.

Power is used to perpetuate and extend existing inequalities. Those in positions of power are able to decide what news is fit to print or air, and what parameters are available for interpreting such news. They decide what books get published, what research is funded and what knowledge is legitimated. Information about people who live in the margins is limited and often distorted through this control.

> **Brenda T.:** I use quotation marks around the word "welfare" because of the way the word is used by the media and other ignorant people to describe us. The word "welfare" when placed in front

of "mother" taints our motherhood, makes us less than human, and less than deserving in the opinion of so many people.

The major institutions, such as the media, educational institutions and government agencies, interpret and choose facts in such a way as to enable them to construct an image of the world that suits their needs. As a result, the facts and interpretations that exist in the public record are restricted and exclusive.

4. We want to demystify the research process and get the word out about the different kinds of knowledge and understanding that methods from the margins can begin to make publicly accessible.

Andrea was hired as a researcher, to study the funding needs of women's centres in Nova Scotia. She was given a research focus which she did not think was the most appropriate for getting at the issues. After discussing this with Sandi, she found a way to change the focus so that it was better able to address the needs of the groups she was investigating while still meeting the goals of those who were funding the project.

During her visits to different communities, women talked with Andrea about the way she was doing the research and expressed interest in gaining access to similar research skills.

Demystifying the research process is the first step in decoding and demythologizing the way knowledge is created. It helps make research skills accessible to those who need them, and enables us to develop a better understanding of the actual social relations and practices that are broadly labelled ideology or culture (Smith, 1984).

5. We believe that researching from the margins is a necessary part of action for change. One student of women's studies wrote:

We have a common belief that there is a lie and that lie is about us.
Our struggle is to realize this, to understand this and change this.

One of the characteristics of oppressed people is that they are often required to perform a kind of doublethink / doublespeak; lies are needed because the truth is not allowed. We believe that research from the margins is necessary in order to begin to share our truths and expose the hidden side of a society that only professes to be democratic and peaceful.

For example, Catherine used the research process as an opportunity to understand her own experience of childhood sexual abuse. At the end of her very personal research project she suggested the possibility of action.

I think I have to make room to turn this topic into action ... the data and myself are begging for such a release. I have a vague picture of myself working with other incest survivors doing research together to help heal ourselves.

6. We hope that the book will provide a point of entry for others who are interested in contributing to research from the margins and the creation of knowledge for change.

Over and over again activists ask, "Where is the work that looks at how social change is brought about?" They point out that although

> how-to-do-it manuals provide step-by-step guidelines for doing almost every human activity, from baking a cake and playing tennis to having a happy relationship and running a war ... there are no such model frameworks available to help activists understand and organize social movements. The lack of a practical how-to-do-it model framework has contributed to some of the most critical common problems of activists and their movements. (Moyer,1986)

Maria Mies has suggested that "separation from praxis" is "one of the most important structural prerequisites" of the academic paradigm (1983:124). What is particularly noteworthy is that while descriptions of the research process emphasize data gathering and analysis, rarely is there any discussion of responsibility to act on what is known. In fact, the opposite seems to be the case. Within the institutions of western education we are trained as spectators or commentators, to absorb experience, not to act on it. This disdain for the practical, an academic paradigm that is particularly strong within the social sciences, has resulted in a kind of paralysis.

There has recently been a great deal of discussion about the political nature of knowledge creation. However, there has been little discussion about how these insights could be translated into actual research practices.

Doing research is a human activity. When we engage in research we involve ourselves in a process in which we construct meaning. Because the social world is multifaceted (i.e. the same situation or experience is able to give us many different kinds of knowledge), when we "do research" we involve ourselves in a process of revealing "possible knowledges" (Morgan, 1983). What knowledge we are able to observe and reveal is directly related to our vantage point, to where we stand in the world. Our interaction with the social world is affected by such variables as gender, race, class, sexuality, age, physical ability, etc. This does not mean that facts about the social world do not exist, but that what we see and how we go about constructing meaning is a matter of interpretation.

For example: quantum physicists have shown, in relation to the study of light, that it is possible to look at light as either a wave or a particle, and that whether light is seen to behave as a wave or as a particle depends on the way it is studied. What is interesting is that if we think about light in the form of a wave we cannot see it in the form of particles. They are mutually exclusive views. "Hence in attempting to study light in one way the scientist precludes the possibility of knowing it in another" (Morgan, 1983:389).

Researching from the margins accepts that:

1. knowledge is socially constructed;
2. social interactions form the basis of social knowledge;
3. different people experience the world differently;
4. because they have different experience people have different knowledge;
5. knowledge changes over time;
6. differences in power have resulted in the commodification of knowledge and a monopoly on knowledge production.

Research from the margins involves more than just learning and then using a set of mechanical skills. While some researchers may argue that research methodologies are like a set of tools from which you can pick and choose depending on the circumstances, we believe that different methodologies carry with them specific underlying assumptions which will shape the way information is gathered and the kind of knowledge created. Dorothy Smith has made an analogy that captures this well. She draws a comparison between those who work "within established methods of thinking and inquiry" and the driver of a car: "It is true that we can do the driving and can choose the direction and destination; but the way the car is put together, how it works, and how and where it will travel structures our relation to the world we travel in" (Smith, 1979:158).

In the conclusion of their book *Making The Difference*, a report on research about educational inequality, Connell et al. stress the need for research to be "organized in a fundamentally different way – by and with the people it is ultimately supposed to benefit." While they acknowledge the very real constraints which hinder such a development (funding, professional commitments, information control), they go on to suggest:

> ... the goal of a different model of research is clear. It should empower the people who are normally just the objects of research, to develop their capacity to research their own situations and evolve their own solutions. It should embody a relationship where expertise is a resource available to all rather than a form of power for a few. (Connell et al., 1982:216)

We hope that this book will contribute to this development.

HOW WE WROTE THE BOOK

As with the development of any knowledge, this has been a collaborative effort. During the past two years, women's studies students at Mount Saint Vincent University (Halifax, Nova Scotia) have been essential collaborators. The examples that we use throughout the book come from their research projects. The insights which they shared have contributed to both our understanding and our commitment to the process of researching from the margins. You will find their names and a description of their research projects in the appendix at the back of the book.

Part of what it means to do research from the margins is that as different people use the method they contribute to the way in which it is developed. We think of research from the margins as method in process; it is continually unfolding. Writing this book is an integral part of this emergent process.

CONTEXTUALIZING THE BOOK

> The right to free expression of ideas and free access to information is a basic human right, and in principle it is available to all, though in practice only to the extent that one has the special privilege, power, training and facilities to exercise these rights in a meaningful way. (Chomsky, 1981:139)

A theme that you will find throughout this book is that of the construction of knowledge as a political process. The fact that universities and research institutes are still largely the domain of white, middle and upper class males can be perceived as a clear manifestation of inequality. However, what may be less obvious is the way choice of research areas, research "rules of the road," and control of research methodology and funding help to construct and legitimate their power and maintain current social relations. The institutionalization of the research process has, in effect, put a monopoly on the creation of certain kinds of knowledge. Demystifying the research process is a way of challenging this monopoly.

It is important to be conscious, throughout the entire research process, of any potential threat the research could pose to the research participants or other marginalized people. Because of their vulnerability and the real possibilities that research information could be used against them, researchers like Susan George argue that research concerned with social change should focus on the rich and powerful and not on those on the margins. She says: "Let the poor study themselves. They already know what is wrong with their lives and if you truly want to help them, the best you can do is give them an idea of how their oppressors are working now and can be expected to work in the future" (1976:289).

While we agree that research on the rich and powerful is essential, we argue that subordinate groups have been structurally blocked from the process of selecting, naming, disseminating and evaluating knowledge. Knowledge production "reflects both the distribution of power and the principles of social control" (Bernstein, quoted in Spender, 1981:3); this process helps to construct and perpetuate current power relations. Researching from the margins is a resource for the oppressed to study themselves. By beginning with the experience and research needs of those who have been silenced, the process of knowledge production is transformed and the ideological power base is challenged.

It has been our experience that people on the margins often know something is wrong, but their concerns are interpreted as a personal problem or failing rather than as a public issue. The method of researching from the margins involves two interrelated processes which connect the personal and political. First, research from the margins requires intersubjectivity: an authentic dialogue between all participants in the research process in which all are respected as equally knowing subjects. And second, it requires critical reflection. Critical reflection involves an examination of people's social reality, for as Freire has pointed out, this is "the real, concrete context of facts" (1985:51).

Research from the margins is not research **on** people from the margins, but research **by, for,** and **with** them. Research from the perspective of the margins will often focus on the oppressors. This can be particularly useful work for those who do not share the experience, but want to act in solidarity with a specific group on the margins. If you undertake such a project, we would stress that it is essential to collaborate with those people on the margins who may benefit from or who may be affected by your research. The insights and direction they can give are invaluable.

There is a larger social context for the book which has four components.

First, there is the academic context. Parts of this book have been presented at conferences and discussed with conference participants. Also, we have prepared a chapter for another book, describing how demystifying research skills helps to bridge the gap between academia and the community. Within this academic context, there is a certain amount of "gatekeeping" (Smith, 1987:26), with sanctions levied against those who challenge the status quo. For example, we found some academic colleagues questioning our collaboration as authors, since within academia joint authorship is not usually regarded as being as strong a publication reference as is a one-author book, and collaboration between a professor and a student is viewed with suspicion. When the idea of the book was first conceived, there was no question that it needed to be written by two authors, one who was more of an academic and the other who was more of an activist.

Second, there is a community context. People who are active in creating social change have been enthusiastic in expressing to us their need for a "how-to" resource to enable them to do research for themselves. They have commented to us throughout the writing of the book on various parts of the process, specifically its usefulness, egalitarianism and sensitivity to people's research needs.

Third, there is a public context. The production and distribution of this book has to meet the research needs of those involved in making social change. Garamond Press has a mandate for producing small, affordable and politically progressive books. Our book will join others of that ilk.

Fourth, there is a personal context. Our friends have encouraged us to formalize, in some way, the information we have about creating knowledge. Neither of us has written a book before and we found the task a daunting one. We have struggled with how best to communicate the dynamism of researching from the margins in a way that would live on a printed page. Our working relationship as co-authors has been an interesting and thoughtful process.

It is within this larger social context that the book has, over time, taken shape.

SOME QUESTIONS THE BOOK ADDRESSES:

- How can we begin to research from our own experience, become our own experts?
- How can we gather data that can provide what we want to know?
- What are the social, political and personal issues involved in creating useful knowledge?
- What are the data gathering and personal skills we need?
- Who has the experience / information?
- How do we analyze large amounts of data in a way that lets it speak?
- How can we use research to get us where we want to go?

Glossary of Terms

Being Honourable:
Throughout the book we talk about "being honourable," "listening to our instincts" and "being authentic." Be assured we are not recommending another "theory of good conduct." One of the characteristics of living in the margins is that we are often required to perform a kind of doublethink / doublespeak. "Being honourable" in the research process means openly recognizing our experience of marginalization and using it as our touchstone. What we are calling for is an exploration of that part of what we know which usually gets left out when our experience is translated into the language of the status quo.

When we say that this kind of research requires that we "listen to our instincts," we are talking about purposefully recognizing / embracing the contradictions and questions that often make us most uncomfortable. We believe Susan Griffin is right in suggesting they may be a gift of knowledge in disguised form (1982).

Collaborators:
A person who does not necessarily have research experience per se but who has a wealth of experience in relation to the research question – one who can greatly assist the researcher.

Collaborators can become special confidants, people who help us focus and assist in keeping various stages of data gathering in order. They can also help us avoid pitfalls and keep us honest in the face of amassing data. Some feminist researchers have suggested that research participants need to become full collaborators in the research process.

Conceptual Baggage:
Conceptual baggage is a record of your thoughts and ideas about the research question at the beginning and throughout the research process. It is a process by which you can state your personal assumptions about the topic and the research process. Recording your conceptual baggage will add another dimension to the data, one that is always present, but rarely acknowledged. By making your thoughts and experience explicit, another layer of data is revealed for investigation. The researcher becomes another subject in the research process and is left vulnerable in a way that changes the traditional power dynamics / hierarchy that has existed between researcher and those who are researched.

Doing Research:
Look at the difference between the words "theory," "research," "knowledge," and the phrases "doing theory," "doing research," "creating knowledge." When we speak about "doing theory," "doing research" or "creating knowledge," we make it obvious that these are human activities which involve intentional activity (Ng, 1987). Speaking in this way allows us to emphasize that doing research is an activity which takes place "in a specific time and place and is engaged in by a specifically located individual, with a specific background, in a specific situation, for a particular series of ends" (Said, 1981:156).

Emergent Research:
Research from the margins is, by its very nature, emergent. We think of it as a method in process; it is continually unfolding. As people use it, what they discover in the process about the process contributes to what we know about research from the margins.

Field Notes:
A researcher's field notes are similar to a journal or drawing. Accordingly, field notes contain written documentation of various aspects of qualitative research: observations, conversations, maps, plans, reflections, memos, preliminary analysis, etc. These notes are, in effect, the "data" on which a substantial part of the analysis and interpretation of the study is based. "The importance of field notes cannot be over-estimated" (J. Golec, Sept. 1984, personal communication).

Hermeneutic of Suspicion:
Shelley Davis Finson makes the point that interpretation of data "requires a critical consciousness which recognizes the systemic nature and ideological dimension of oppression." She suggests there is a need for this "hermeneutic

of suspicion" in the process of interpretation *"not* in regard to the words of the women, but rather in regard to the *context* within which and out of which they are functioning" (1985:115-117).

Ideology:

"The concept of ideology provides us with a thread through the maze different from our more familiar notion of 'culture,' for it directs us to look for and at the actual practical organization of the production of images, ideas, symbols, concepts and vocabularies, as means for us to think about our world. It directs us to examine who produces what for whom, where the social forms of consciousness come from" (Smith, 1987:54).

Information Monopoly / Research Monopoly:

The fact that universities and research institutes are still largely the domain of white, middle and upper class males can be perceived as a clear manifestation of inequality. What may be less obvious is the way choice of research areas, research "rules of the road," and control of research methodology help to construct and legitimate their power. The institutionalization of the research process has, in effect, put a monopoly on the creation of knowledge.

> The right to free expression of ideas and free access to information is a basic human right, and in principle it is available to all, though in practice only to the extent that one has the special privilege, power, training and facilities to exercise these rights in a meaningful way. (Chomsky, 1981:139)

The Margins:

The margin is the context in which those who suffer injustice, inequality and exploitation live their lives. People find themselves on the margins not only in terms of the inequality in the distribution of material resources, but also knowledge production is organized so that the views of a small group of people are presented as objective, as "The Truth." The majority of people are excluded from participating as either producers or subjects of knowledge.

One of the characteristics of living in the margins is the frequent necessity to perform a kind of doublethink / doublespeak in order to translate our experience into acceptable and understandable terms for the status quo.

Focussing on the world from the perspective of the margins allows us to see the world differently and, in many ways, more authentically.

Method:

The way in which we gather information and analyze it. All methods are value laden; they contain implicit assumptions about the world. Different research methods are in fact different ways of classifying people and organizing the world.

Positivism:

> ... a way of seeing and constructing the world, which insists that "physical" and "social" worlds are in all essentials the same. Positivism claims that in any occurrence there is one true set of events ("the facts") which is discoverable by reference to witnesses and material evidence of other kinds.... It describes social reality as "objectivity constituted" and so insists that there is one true "real" reality. And it suggests that researchers can find out this reality because they remove themselves from involvement in what they study. (Stanley and Wise, 1983:193-94).

Power:

Power appears in different forms. One definition is that power is the probability that an individual or group will be able to carry out its will even against resistance (Weber). However, Westergaard and Resler argue that real confusion can arise if the term "power" is used only when speaking of dominance that subdues opposition, while dominance that is "legitimized" by lack of opposition is spoken of as "authority." Not only does the word authority "convey a misleading notion of dominance both less absolute and more beneficent than 'power'," but "no control could be firmer and more extensive than one which embraced the minds and will of its subjects so successfully that opposition never even reared its ugly head" (1975:145).

Praxis:

Praxis is thoughtful reflection and action that occurs simultaneously. Praxis is the integration of knowing and doing.

The Process:

Research from the margins involves two interrelated processes. First, research from the margins requires **intersubjectivity**: an authentic dialogue between all participants in the research process in which all are respected as equally knowing subjects.

Second, it requires **critical reflection**. Without reflection and analysis of the social context, research remains merely functional, enabling people to function within the status quo rather than to interact with and change social relations. Critical reflection involves an examination of the social reality in which people exist, for as Paulo Freire has pointed out, this is "the real, concrete context of facts" (1985:51).

Rage:
A sense of outrage and anger can be enabling in doing research. While status quo researchers may describe the social world as an interesting thing to study, people on the margins often have a compelling need to do research because they find the status quo so outrageous, inequitable and unsatisfying.

Reliability:
Reliability refers to the trust or confidence we have when speaking about the description and analysis of our data. Does our description truly represent what we found? Is it true? Can the description or analysis be depended on? Are research participants able to see their experience in the research report?

Research:
"Re-search," according to Webster's Dictionary, means "to search or investigate again." Throughout this book we use the word "research" knowing it includes everything from re-search, to searching, to making sense of.... Just as we recognize that it is not only teachers who teach, not only cartographers who create maps, we use the word "research" as a familiar word, reclaiming the understanding that research is something we all do in our everyday lives. Doing research means gathering and making sense of information and acting responsibly with that information.

Research Participant:
One who has the experience that has been identified as the focus of the research and who is willing to share her / his understanding of that experience with researchers. Research participants may also be collaborators and researchers. That is, participants can collaborate with researchers on the way in which research is done (questions asked, focus of analysis, identification of other participants). Participants can also be involved in the organization and reporting of a research project. In all instances, participants and researchers have equal status, are equally important.

The Ruling Apparatus / Relations of Ruling:
These concepts come from the work of Dorothy Smith. When she uses the term "ruling," she is "identifying a complex of organizational practices, including government, law, business and financial management, professional organization, and educational institutions as well as the discourses in texts that interpenetrate the multiple sites of power. A mode of ruling has become dominant that involves a continual transcription of the local and particular actualities of our lives into abstracted and generalized forms" (1987:3).

Theory:
"Theories reflect the political world views of the people writing them: how they see the world, where they think it ought to go, as well as how they see that happening and the direction it should move in" (J. quoted in Kate's research project).

Thought Cloth:
A thought cloth is a web of information that has a particular texture, density and colour reflecting the unique perspective of its creator.

Validity:
For our research to be valid, we must be able to say that what we describe is recognized by the research participants as so. We might ask whether the material really says what we think it says. What do collaborators and research participants understand the research descriptions and explanations to be?

SCHEMA

PREPARATION

Identify research interest
Find a research focus
Do your conceptual baggage

PLANNING

Refocus your question
Identify options for data gathering
Draw up research plan
Identify research participants

DATA GATHERING

Prepare to gather data
Gather and record data
Reflect on data
Reflect on process

ANALYSIS

Organize the data
Code the data
Describe codes and categories
Describe links between categories
Develop and refine analysis

ACTION

Prepare draft report
Share draft report with research participants
Review and revise draft into final report
Get the word out
Translate knowledge gained through research into action

Part Two

Getting Ready

Reasearching from the Margins:
The Process
getting ready ✔
getting focussed
gearing up for data gathering
planning for data gathering
gathering data
preparing for and doing analysis
presenting the data

INTRODUCTION

Chapter One is intended as a practical starting point as you begin doing your research. You can start here and, by using the following chapters as a how-to guide, begin to focus, find a research question, gather information, analyze the data you collect and produce a report of your findings. The research process we describe developed through use and in collective dialogue with others. We hope that as you engage in your own research, you will challenge, clarify and add to this emergent process.

We do not believe that research is solely the domain of the academics. Since creation of knowledge is the business of research, and since knowledge can be used as a tool of control, it is in the best interests of those outside the relations of ruling (see Glossary), specifically those on the margins (see Introduction), to engage in the production of knowledge.

We believe research activities should empower the people who are usually merely the objects of research. It therefore does not make sense to use paradigms and rules created by those with an interest in maintaining the status quo. We need to be aware, through all the different stages, exactly how the research process is being organized through choice of research areas, research "rules of the road," and control over methodology.

Choosing the method for a particular piece of research is a political process. Deciding how the research will be done and who or what will be studied
entails making choices. These choices often incorporate assumptions which
the researcher takes for granted, such as who is important to study, what
context of research is identified, what data gathering method is best and
who is most qualified to engage in research.

For example, a major problem with much of the research that has been
done to date is the omission of women from the data. The following
examples illustrate the seriousness of the problem:

> Example 1: In his research on developmental ages and stages, Erick-
> son (1963) originally used boys as subjects. He made the assumption
> that little boys and little girls experience the same stages. Girls' expe-
> rience was not part of his original research sample and yet his results
> were generalized to both girls and boys. Erickson both misrepre-
> sented and marginalized girls.

> Example 2: A review of sport retirement literature reveals a heavy
> concentration on male athletes as research subjects and a general-
> ization of the research results to include *all* athletes, female and
> male (Kirby, 1986:22). If attention is not paid to the gender of high
> performance athletes, the research is gender blind. Ultimately, this
> leads to the misrepresentation of women's experience as athletes
> and as women leaving high performance sport.

These are just two examples of many that illustrate the need for critical analysis of the context in which research is done, the people for whom the
research speaks, as well as the underlying assumptions of such research.
Shelley Davis Finson calls this process of critical interpretation the "hermeneutic of suspicion" (1985) (see Glossary). This suspicion leads ultimately
to a different kind of research, different questions being asked – the questions would not deal simply with women's lives but with women's lives
within the context of a patriarchal world.

Why certain approaches to gathering data are chosen often goes
unquestioned, even unmentioned. But when researching from the margins it
is important to clearly account for **how and why** the research is being done,
and **who** is being researched. For example:

> I was a member of the 1976 Olympic rowing team. When I left high
> performance sport in 1981, it was because I could not continue to
> focus my energies and attention on the sport at the level required to

remain competitive. Removing the many layers of being an athlete took some time. Because of these experiences, I have chosen to examine the retirement of the 1976 female Olympians. My research self overlaps with my athlete self, and it is the blending of these skills and experiences which colour my research and my writing. (Kirby, 1986:ix)

In this way, the researcher is incorporated into the research and is not left hidden from the process.

WHAT IS RESEARCH?

Researching is like embarking on a voyage of discovery. As the voyage takes place, the researcher maps or charts the process of exploration. For example, if you were to explore Canada and create your own maps as you went, you would be doing research. The paradigm (*what* is to be studied and *what rules* are to be used) might indicate that Canada is a country of so many square kilometres, bounded by the border to the south, the western shore, a northern boundary and an eastern shore. How can this territory be best explored? You might choose to use only public roads. You would then limit your exploration to those areas where roads have been established. You would not be able to access many remote communities. Given these restraints, you might choose to explore the country in different ways. Choices must be made about what parts of the country are more important to explore than others and how you can record what you are observing on your explorations. The rules you choose will both limit and enable you to do your research.

Another approach to doing research is to replicate someone else's research. In our current example, this means that you would take maps already created by some other researcher and travel the same routes making your own observations. In all likelihood, because you are a different person than the original researcher, you will make unique observations.

Good research includes making observations, recording them fully, reporting on them in an understandable way and distributing the information to others. Suppose you record your observations by drawing a map. There are many different ways of drawing observational maps ... as many ways as there are ways of observing. A map with clear descriptions and conclusions would be better than one that consists of speculations. Good maps provide enough information to adequately describe, explain and generate further questions about the mapped areas. Poor maps are those which are decipherable by only a few people and which do not describe the terrain clearly enough to be of easy use.

A researcher needs the skills of an explorer: good eyes, good ears, a clear mind and a vision of the land to be explored. The researcher also needs a method for recording her / his observations and a facility for constructing good "maps." In addition, creators of new information must outline why a particular method has been chosen to study the particular research question (this is the process by which the researcher accounts for her / his personal experience that led to the research undertaking). The researcher should not shy away from the experience being studied – the more familiar with the experience the researcher is, the better potential understanding of it she / he will have.

Everyone who does research is essentially doing science, that is, creating knowledge. The systematic application of a few principles of observation and analysis, principles which we all use in everyday life, can enable us to create knowledge. It is to be noted that being systematic does *not* free a researcher from bias. It must always be remembered that research tools have been developed by people who see the world in particular ways. Every time a research tool is used, the researcher must be aware that it contains the bias of its creators.

Researching from the margins is a continuous process that begins with a concern that is rooted in experience. The research process consists of planning to gather information, actually gathering it and making sense of it; concurrently the researcher engages in a process of self-reflection as one of the participants in the process of creating knowledge.

BEGINNING THE PROCESS
This section details the first three steps in doing research from the margins: identifying your research interest, identifying your specific question, and recording your conceptual baggage (see Glossary). Each is discussed in turn.

1) Identifying your research interest
It is usually difficult to start a research project. Until the central focus of the research is clear, planning the research is next to impossible. Imagine writing a letter of complaint to the federal government without knowing what the nature of the complaint is. It is just as difficult to begin doing research without the central focus being clear.[1]

Finding the focus means identifying those questions you might be interested in gathering information about. There are many reasons why a particular research focus might be more attractive than others:

---

1. Early on in the research process, it is important to describe the research focus even if only in vague outline form. From the schema of the research plan (see Introduction), you can see that there is a place for refocussing the question.

- your community might **need information** on use of the local playground;

- you live in a remote area and only **certain kinds of information are available**;

- the group you're working with formed around a **particular interest** in the federal abortion law.

What are you interested in researching? Start by first locating yourself in the general topics in which you are interested. To do this, you can map out possible research concerns and the experience you have in relation to those concerns. It won't be a complete mapping, but it will form the parameters within which your research can begin to take shape. In researching from the margins, your experience guides the way the research is done and how it is understood: your experience is at the centre of the research process.

The following steps will help you get underway.

a) What is it that you want to find out more about?
The answer to this question is the beginning of your research focus and will lead to the research question. Identifying your research focus may be straightforward or it may be a complex process. If you are doing individual research, in all likelihood the concerns that you are interested in researching will arise from your own experience.[2] For example, Sandi, in her research, wanted to know how other female Olympians left high performance competition. The concern did not come out of a vacuum but emerged from her own experience and from the absence of women in the data she read. In other words, Sandi **already knew a lot about the topic experientially before she started to research**.

It might help you to sit, pen in hand (or in front of a computer or a tape recorder, or with a friend) and begin to consider what it is you, as an individual, are interested in researching. If you have a relatively clear idea already, this exercise will simply define the area of concern more accurately.

If you want to gain some research experience but have no idea what to research, think of the broad areas of interest you have. These might be:

---

2. If you are working on a group project, it is valuable for each of your group members to write (or record by some other means) a rough research focus before meeting as a group to negotiate a more refined definition. In this way, the individual voices get heard and group collaboration for the duration of the research project can be established right from the start. Try to identify what you already know about the project (funding, duration, possible research plans, your personal involvement) in addition to **what you think needs to be researched**.

local politics, the battered women's shelter, dependency on government funding, racism, children's books without violence, the family
tree, your grandfather's (grandmother's) life story, long term lesbian
(gay, heterosexual) relationships, going back to school, learning to
read better, a niece's dependency on drugs, homelessness, Native
land claims, aging, uranium mining....

Think about topics, mull them over in your mind, figure out which ones
attract you more, which ones you can imagine trying to gather information
on. The topic area you choose does not have to be the one you already know
most about. It can be the one you have the greatest curiosity about or the
one that you know you want to do something about. However, in the long
run, it is helpful if you can find a research focus that you feel some attach-
ment to. Such emotive energy will stand you in good stead as you progress
through the research process. Often, talking through your ideas with someone else can give you a clearer idea of what it is you **really want to do**.

Remember that who you are has a central place in the research process
because you bring your own thoughts, aspirations and feelings, and your
own ethnicity, race, class, gender, sexual orientation, occupation, family
background, schooling, etc., to your research. Also, remember that doing
research is an entire process beginning with finding a focus through to acting
on what you know. This beginning part of research is called **starting where
you are** (Lofland and Lofland, 1984).

Think of finding a research focus as the first of many steps and remember that you are only taking one step at a time. You will be unable to predict
the final outcome until you are actually engaged in the analysis and writing.
It is best not to dwell on the final product or worry about how you're going to
do the final writing. Rather, think about each step as you go, one small step
at a time.

b) Focussing
A description of your research focus could take several forms. It could be in
the form of a statement of direction. For example, Lorene's focus was clear
right from the beginning: "I came to the class knowing I wanted / needed to
explore spirituality and, in particular, feminist spirituality." Or, it could be in
the form of a general area of interest. For example, Sarah knew she wanted
to focus on lesbianism but was unable to state a refined question until after
she had done more thinking about it. Later in her research, just before she
began gathering data, she settled on **the research question**: "Why are explanations of lesbianism necessary and for whom?" However, at this first stage
of the process, all you need is a rough idea of the direction in which you are
going.

c) Living with the general focus

You have lived with your very general focus for a short time now. Ask yourself a) does it feel comfortable? b) does it feel uncomfortable? c) is it really the focus I want to take? and d) is it "right on" or does it feel as if it is not quite right? If you are feeling and thinking positively about the research focus and have a certain comfort with the way in which you have expressed it, you are ready to move along to the next step, doing conceptual baggage. If you are not, then it is important for you to re-examine the general focus. Ask yourself "Is this really what I want to focus on?" "Is there a different approach to this that allows more room to explore the *topic*?" "Is this really what is needed?" You may want to go back over the three steps to get better settled with the description of your research interest.

2) Framing your question

Refining the research topic involves framing a question that will guide you through the research. It is difficult to find the best question and, at times, you might not be able to clarify the question fully until you are further along in the process. Traditional research stresses the necessity of framing a single question before beginning to gather any data. The process of researching from the margins is more flexible. Occasionally the questions may emerge from the research or crystallize through the process. At other times a specific question may actually hinder the data gathering. For example, Catherine found that she needed a broad research focus in order to explore her own experience as an incest survivor. However, usually you will find that the more concise the question, the easier it will be to keep focussed throughout the process. So too, because of the large volume of data that you will gather, a concise question makes it easier when you begin to do your analysis. Therefore, it is worth spending time to clarify your research question near the beginning of your research.

Here are some other examples of how various researchers framed their research questions. The original context of the research is provided.

Helen Roberts tackled the problem of invisibility of women. Her research (with Michele Barrett) centred on the fact that women see their doctor more frequently than men do. Her questions allowed for an analysis of whether the visits are psychosomatically or sociosomatically induced.

> We wanted to explore the possibility that women in this position (disadvantaged educationally, economically and in other ways), particularly women with little interest outside their families, use their doctors as a source of attention and sympathy as well as a source of compensation for the frustrations and inadequacies of their daily lives. (Roberts, 1981:10)

Doris Marshall expressed a great sadness at the agonizing slowness of change in dealing with the needs of those who are older. She was angry that some of the so-called advances are not really advances from the perspective of the elderly.

> I have chosen to write about old age and old people as we approach the twenty-first century. I hope that in so doing it will be possible to see, through the prism of my lifetime, how the way we live our lives has changed over the years, and what must be done if old people are, in fact, to see themselves and be seen as persons of worth and value. (Marshall, 1988:14)

Brian Miller wrote about the problems of gay familymen in being parents and living a gay lifestyle. He was interested in the way in which gay identity is formed and how that is related to being gay familymen. He wanted "to explore the identity patterns of gay familymen" (Miller, 1983:1).

These examples show researchers beginning with a *problem or concern*. All three research questions are worded differently.

Many researchers start with a specific research question that then changes over time. For example, Susan Krieger presents an absorbing account of her year in a women's community. She gathered data through interviews and participant observation, and only determined what her specific research focus was after the data had been gathered.

> Individual identity in a women's community.... I originally intended to study privacy ... in time, however, I came to understand that my inquiries into privacy required me to explore dilemmas of identity ... I came to be concerned about control over definition of self. (Krieger, 1983:xi)

Liz Stanley and Sue Wise write at length about their experiences with obscene telephone calls. These calls came when their telephone number became the contact for a lesbian group. Although Stanley and Wise did not plan to do such research, they took the opportunity and produced important new knowledge.

> Our experiences with obscene phone calls weren't produced as part of any academic exercise. Their occurrence was linked to our involvement in the gay movement in Britain.... We spent a great deal of our lives thinking about the obscene calls and in particular what they told us about the nature of oppression.... (Stanley and Wise, 1983:198-99)

If you do not have a lot of research experience, you will find the task easier if you work with a well defined research question. Framing a **concise and**

clear question is important since good research comes from focussed questions. Even the most experienced researchers often find framing just the right question difficult. However, if you frame the question well, it will help to maintain your focus throughout the remainder of the research process.

Some suggestions to help you:

- choose a question that has enough research scope but not so much that it cannot be answered;
- choose a question that you are able to gather information about;
- choose a question that is exciting or enticing. It has to be able to sustain your interest and maintain the research focus throughout the research process;
- choose a question that comes from your experience; your biography is central to how you have come to ask the question and to why you want answers to it.

Talk to someone else about what it is you want to do. In doing this, the question may well begin to clarify.

It is not essential that your research focus be associated with your personal problems, troubles or concerns. Research opportunities may appear spontaneously and they "should be gratefully grasped and fully explored" (Stanley and Wise, 1983: 207). But remember, whether the question is personal or public in nature, it must be *important* to you.

3) The conceptual baggage: how to do it

Conceptual baggage is the record of the experience and reflections of the researcher that relate to the focus of the research (see Glossary). Since all research is done by someone, it is essential that that "someone" is identified in some way and accounted for in the research. One way to do the accounting is to record both the research you are doing and your reflections on it as you move through the research process.

In all research, it is necessary to record both the information sought and gathered (the content) and how the research is done (the process). In researching from the margins, conceptual baggage is a large part of that record. It consists primarily of jottings about the topic or the process and ongoing reflections throughout the research enterprise.

Initially, the conceptual baggage is a way of focussing on a topic. Later, the conceptual baggage consists of your reflections on the content and process of the research, any preliminary conclusions you see, any interesting and unexpected links that appear, difficulties you have or solutions as they come to you. These reflections can keep you focussed, keep numerous bits of information organized and even keep your creativity vibrant.

The recording is best done in a systematic way. Record the conceptual baggage either in a separate file or book. Draw a margin down the centre of the pages in the file or use facing pages of a notebook. Dated entries will be written on one side of the page or notebook; the additional space is left as a margin in which you can comment or reflect on these entries as your research progresses.

Content	Reflections
I haven't read anything about the topic. Along the same lines I haven't read anything on parenting or mothering. Growing up, most of my ideas were borrowed from my brothers and sisters. In recent years it has become a priority to understand MY reaction to things before I adopt anyone else's ideas.	except perhaps some ideas I have come across accidently while reading a magazine identity starting where I am

At the start of your research, recording your conceptual baggage will help formulate the question or raise concerns you might have about being a researcher. For example, Catherine went back to her journals to find references related to incest. It soon became apparent to her that everything was related. Rather than look at published works to find out about incest, she concentrated on the examination of her own experience. Some of this was conceptual baggage (what she thought and felt) and some was experiential observations recorded when she was a little girl. From this she was able to formulate a research focus which incorporated the data and her grown-up response to it.

The conceptual baggage includes both intellectual thinking and emotional comments; it is like an ongoing diary of you and your research woven together. Being cognizant of the relationship between the thinking and the emotional part is important because you will likely find yourself "going on instinct" in this research. It is your way of keeping your own experience and process observable and accounted for in the investigation.

> **Tarel:** Writing my conceptual baggage was a fascinating, hilarious, depressing, horrifying and liberating experience. Seeing my pre-conceived ideas in ink gave me the opportunity to distance myself from them and critically evaluate them.

Writing your conceptual baggage allows you to identify, at a later point in the research, whether any pre-established goals, assumptions or responsibilities may be overly influencing how your research is developing. For example, Robbie was interested in describing and explaining how the International Women's Day events were organized on her campus. She began by reflecting on her own expectations and previous involvement with I.W.D. committees. As she wrote, she identified her involvement, values, beliefs and experience as they related to the research topic. This acted as a touchstone for her, a touchstone to which she constantly returned to account for herself in the research process. Her final analysis of her research included her reflections on how she interacted with the other research participants and with the data gathered. This is what she wrote:

> After interviewing the three women, it was obvious that they shared many similarities including age, feelings and recent naming of themselves as feminists. I had not consciously chosen these three women for their similarities, and for awhile I felt a strong need to interview other committee members. I felt uneasy about the time constraints which prevented me from interviewing other women on the committee, but I realized that I was creating problems by trying to shape my data to my own expectations rather than accepting and working with the voices I had. Discovering this, I felt a strong commitment to allowing all three voices equal weight with my own in shaping the research.

Having written her conceptual baggage, Robbie was able to reflect on her reaction to the data in a way she might not have otherwise.

Your conceptual baggage might include such things as the problem you want to know more about followed by several pages of free flowing thought on what you think you already know, gaps in what you know, questions you might want to ask, and your certainties and uncertainties about doing the research. Your conceptual baggage might also include a self description or a description of your world view. Try answering questions such as:

What is it in my experience that leads me to be interested in this research topic?
How does my experience contribute to or inform this research?

Throughout the research enterprise, who you are as a person, including the particular experience you have, affects what you can know.

The writing of conceptual baggage is part of the research process from the very beginning. As you move through the research process, you will find it useful to go back to your conceptual baggage and rethink certain thoughts or beliefs you wrote down. This new perspective on "old" ideas is again written in your conceptual baggage. This exercise is called **layering**. Layering can be done several times over the same material, as new insights are gained about process and content. Layering also allows you to continually account for yourself in the process, including things like decisions you make and the reasons you make them, any thoughts you might have about doing research and what other people tell you about the research when you talk to them about it.[3]

As we, the authors, have used this research process, we have become aware of how external parameters can organize and influence our work as researchers and the knowledge we create. Because of this, we would suggest that as well as recording your personal conceptual baggage and reflections, you also need to acknowledge the historical / political context in which the research occurs. You can do this by asking if any pre-established goals, assumptions or responsibilities influence or organize your work. This is important, for these questions reveal the "forms of consciousness that are properties of organization and relations [of ruling] rather than individuals" (Smith, 1987:220).

Earlier, you sought to identify what the focus of your research might be. After writing some of your conceptual baggage, you will have a more lively sense of your topic and of your interest in it. If you are still not very focussed, it is best to spend some time focussing before moving further into the research process.

---

3. If you are part of a group doing research, in addition to the personal conceptual baggage, you should together map out your group's role in the research. You can begin to do this by answering questions such as: "How do we see ourselves doing this particular research?" "What are our initial concerns about being researchers?" "What range of experience have we with the research topic and the process of doing research?" and "What do we want to accomplish with this research?" Such stock-taking provides you with an overall grasp of your starting points.

SUMMARY AND CHECKPOINTS

This chapter is a practical starting point for you as you begin to do research. As you make choices about how you do the research and who you study, your personal thoughts and feelings get involved. This chapter helps you to focus on an area of interest, examine whether it feels right, and then begin the difficult process of **finding** a question. The chapter explains the importance of acknowledging the existence of conceptual baggage.

The main theme of this first chapter is that it is essential to state your assumptions and thereby contextualize yourself in the research. By doing this, you change the traditional power dynamics or the hierarchy which tends to exist between the researcher and those who are researched. The researcher becomes another subject in the research process and another dimension is added to the data. This dimension in the researching process is always present but is rarely made explicit or exposed in traditional research as another layer for investigation.

Checkpoints:
- What does it mean to "start where you are"?
- Am I able to identify, from other researcher's descriptions, how and why various research projects have been done?
- How can I approach data gathering?
    - mapping skills
    - researching skills
- How do I begin the research process?
    - identifying your research interest
    - focussing
    - framing a question
    - doing conceptual baggage
    - content and reflections
- What is layering and why is it important to being an attentive observer?

CHAPTER TWO

Getting Focussed

---

getting ready
getting focussed ✔
gearing up for data gathering
planning for data gathering
gathering data
preparing for and doing analysis
presenting the data

INTRODUCTION

This chapter describes an exercise, a library tour, that will help you practice getting data and reflecting on the data as you are gathering it. This library tour could be any data gathering venture where you go from source to source paying attention to what catches your eye. Later in this chapter, you are shown how your skill at recording conceptual baggage (Chapter One) combined with your skill at reflection will enable you to focus and find the right research question.

There is no such thing as an impartial or unimpassioned researcher. If you were to follow your interests, you would arrive at a different conclusion than others. Rather than consider your interests as limitations of your vision, consider them as enhancements of your vision, built on the diversity of your experience. As we explore ideas, a single piece of research often produces more than one equally plausible conclusion. Rather than debate which is more correct, we believe that it is the diversity of the creators of knowledge that accounts for the diversity of research and understanding about human lives that exists.

GETTING FOCUSSED

1) Freeing up our thinking: the library tour

How can you learn to be attentive, to listen to the voices of those around you? In traditional research, you might begin by going to the library and completing a review of all the available literature on the topic on which you are focussing. But what if you want to understand **how the way you think** will allow you to hear and make sense of certain voices more readily than others? This is what the library tour is about. **It is an experience in thinking freely and reflecting upon how you think.** Being free to think means getting rid of the "shoulds" that tell you how you *should* think, what you *should* gather and where you *should* go for information. It also means understanding that you think differently than anyone else and that it is precisely this unique understanding that enables you to do different research than others. **You** are important to your research task. No one else can do it as you would. If you invest yourself in the research process, and if you do thorough and honourable (see Glossary) research, it will be good research.

Thus, you are invited to play in the library ...

The Library Tour
This library tour is unlike any you may have been taken on. Its goal is to help you figure out **how** you think, how you move from piece to piece of information, how you make links between those pieces of information and how you move from the information to ideas and theories. What you are recording are called field notes. Field notes are an ongoing record of the research. These consist of content (the information you gather) and reflections (thoughts you have about the content and about the process of researching). The exercise of the library tour[1] is to get you used to combining your search for ideas with an understanding of how you think and feel.

You can begin with a single word or idea and follow it wherever your interest takes you for a set period of time, maybe two hours. Once in the library, you could start with the card catalogue: look up the word of interest

---

1. Or a tour of a department store, a local fair or even a trip to a part of your province that is unfamiliar. The library is not the only place where such a tour can occur. The grocery store, a court house or a newspaper are also ready-made data sources.

You could just as easily use this exercise to take a tour of your community. Begin with a focus of interest and follow it for a specific amount of time. Take along a camera or a sketch book and use them to record items that catch your interest. During this time keep a record of what you are thinking. Take notes to fill in the context of your photo or sketch. Record both content (what you stop to look at) and reflections (what you are thinking as you stop, select, record and move along). These reflections are an ongoing record of how your mind works while you are engaged in research. Both content and reflections are integral features of the process of researching from the margins.

you have chosen, jot down two or three books that incorporate that word in their catalogue reference, then locate them on the shelf and flip through their pages. Words, names, dates, ideas will jump out from the pages at you: take note of those items that catch your interest, and continue your search through the library using these new reference points as stepping stones and guides.

Although there is a more detailed discussion later in the chapter, the example provided below shows how you can record your tour. Notice that the entries are dated.

Reflections	Recorded Data
	Jan 16
Who is writing this? What is their point of view?	"The woman's seclusion area, 'Mambasi,' is polluted. It contains the birth hut ... also includes a heap of stones in the lagoon where the woman buries the placenta and where aborted fetuses and children who die in the
Infanticide?	birth hut are buried."
	It also contains menstrual huts, communal cookhouse and women's lavatory.
this is important a fact they constantly try to deny	"no men may enter the women's area, but all men are born in the birth hut."
	ceremonies of purification / / baptism for us

Field work and the library tour are similar. If you stand in a library and look around you, you are actually surrounded by the voices of many authors. You might think of each author's work as the equivalent of someone you might interview or talk with about your research. In each publication, authors are conversing with each other and with you, announcing their positions on various topics, arguing points and describing events (Glassner and Corzine, 1982).

While you tour the library you are creating new information. As your interests lead you to various materials, your own unique sense of them results in new descriptions. Your interests guide what you are able to see, record, make sense of and write about.

In your library tour, you have only to gather what information you like. You are not trying to produce specific research or follow a particular plan. The information is at your disposal, but with no uniform strategy for gathering the information, your own way of thinking becomes the guide.

The library tour can provide many research opportunities. First, after your time in the library, you are sure to have some sense of what the library site looks like. In doing research of any kind, maintaining an overall sense of the site (or experience, or focus) is useful for allowing researchers to look intently at the particular but maintain a sense of the entirety; to see the trees but remember, too, that they are in a forest.

Second, after completing a library tour, you will have some experience as an active creator. That is, your way of gathering and making sense of the information at the data site is unique. The process comes expressly from you. Anyone else could go to that same library site and start at the same spot you began but would produce an entirely different account of their tour. Both are correct, though different.

Third, you will likely have discovered relationships between words or authors or positions of books on shelves that you did not expect to find. These relationships are often exciting and can pull your research in new directions.

And finally, as you explore the library, you become more aware of how you think. How you think can be like weaving a piece of cloth, but not a regular one ... one woven of ideas. This is your **thought cloth** (see Glossary). As you come to know ideas and experiences, you begin to link them together in ways that make sense to you. Eventually, there are threads of thought that you can later weave into a fabric of ideas. The texture, density, colours and patterns you use are all symbolic of the ideas you have linked through your personal understanding. Each researcher weaves differently and will therefore weave a different thought cloth. Just as you can often tell the trademark patterns of certain weavers or potters or painters, you can often identify the trademark patterns of certain researchers.

You may find that rather than weaving a dense thought cloth, you prefer to follow a single strand of thought. The approach you take to information on the tour may well be the same approach you take to gathering information from individuals who have experiences you are interested in exploring.

Here is a sample description of a library tour.

Practical Beginnings

1. Start with a recording sheet(s) divided into two columns:

Reflections	Recorded Data

2. Recording

Starting Point
> the author, subject or point of departure that you have chosen or happened upon

> [for example, start with an author (Woolf, Freire, Gzowski), a subject (birthday, cross-dressing, unions) or a point of departure (first book on the shelf to the left of the fire hose)]

3. Recording

Information
> the steps of your library field work (where you go, what you find)

> [for example, "Start at the author section of the catalogue, go to HQ section of library, pick up first book by Woolf, look at middle of book, word "bluestockings" catches my eye, thumb through three other Woolf books until I find one with an index, look up blue stockings and go to reference section of library to find out ..."]

4. Recording

Conceptual Baggage (Reflections)
> the personal information and links behind how you move

through the data, and how you see yourself as you discover the data

[for example, "I tried not to plan but as soon as I got into the library I knew I would have to appear to be working because that is what everyone else seemed to be doing; I went to the card catalogue and remembered that Virginia Woolf had committed suicide ... so did an uncle of mine, so I went to find out something about her."]

5. Layering

At the end of approximately two hours, you will have a list of data (names, places, new information, connections and more). You will also have a sketchy set of new ideas and thoughts (discoveries) for topics, leisure reading, related topics to explore, some thoughts about the research process. Fill in the reflections in greater detail after you leave the library.

Leave the data and reflections for a day or two, then go back and fill in any additional reflections. This is your chance to reflect on your reflections. If you use different coloured ink or pencils each time you add to these reflections, it will help to illustrate the way your analysis develops over time.

[for example, "I never thought of the library as a place to play but my mind really played. I soon got away from the "shoulds," and just started to enjoy being there; I really do jump from topic to topic and I gathered books as I went, books that had nothing to do with the project but that I thought I might read; I went from Woolf to "Bluestockings" to fashion to fetishism to vanity and ended the two hours with rebellion ..."]

6. Write Up

Conclude the field work with an evaluation of YOUR experiences as an active creator of a web of information that has texture, density and colour. Answer the question "What kind of thought cloth does my mind like to weave?" and comment on the experience.

[for example, "My mind jumps all over the place. I have to admit that the thought cloth I weave is not very dense; in fact, it's full of holes and covers a huge area ... but it is very brightly coloured, only bright, intense topics attract me and I go from place to place because of the feel of the word ... not because it is the next logical place to go...."]

On a cautionary note, the library tour is not to be confused with doing a review of the literature. In more traditional approaches to research, a review of the literature is a prerequisite to setting an hypothesis and to analyzing the data. In the method of researching from the margins, a review of the literature may be done principally to gather information when primary (first hand) information is unavailable, but is not a prerequisite.

We have done a library tour for a different purpose, to find out how our mind works and to practice recording and reflecting skills. Even though library material is accessible and information can be gathered quickly and expediently, there are problems if you use the library as your only source of information. Although many people research in this way, as a researcher interested in social change you cannot observe any interactions that haven't been written about, and many voices are absent in what has been written. Also, you cannot discuss the author's views or add your information to the text. Further, you cannot discover whether the author is accurate. Library material needs at some level to be verified by other methods, other sources of information.

2) Refocussing the question: finding just the right question

Earlier (Chapter One), you tried to identify what the focus of your research might be. After preparation of conceptual baggage and participation in a library tour, the researcher may reevaluate the overall conception of the research project. Recording your conceptual baggage, what you already know about the topic and why it interests you, may have shifted the focus of your question or helped you narrow it down. During the library tour you practiced gathering data and reflecting on what you gathered. It was also an opportunity to discover how your unique vision enhances the research process. With these experiences to guide you, you can begin to take a second look at your research focus.

Here are some examples of how some researchers refocussed their research interest subsequent to doing their conceptual baggage and the library tour.

> **Andrea:** Non-monogamy — I was thinking of studying something that was defined as the absence of something else. Non-monogamy is the absence of monogamy and I certainly didn't want to study monogamy. I was already feeling discomfort with the whole system of terms and categories of relationships that make up popular wisdom. Not only does my life not fit into the patterns, I couldn't even find words that adequately express my reality. Using these reflections, I chose to focus on relationships and the dynamic between the language available to us and the meanings we try to express and explore.

Andrea's first broad focus was non-monogamy. What became clear as she recorded her conceptual baggage, and later chatted with Sandi in an attempt to clarify her question, was that she was focussing on something that had been defined as the absence of something else. Since this was part of what she saw as the problem it enabled her to focus in on the connection between language and relationships.

> **Tarel:** Diamonds are a girl's best friend.... Initially I felt my research topic was trite since it did not deal with crucial issues such as wife battering or sexual abuse. But I am having a real struggle with the feeling that I do not fit into my age group. I really want to know how girls grow up thinking that all they have to do is find some man and then all their worries will be over. What about afterwards? What about the reality of Canada's divorce rate?

During three years at university, Tarel's ideas had changed drastically and she felt she no longer fit into her age group. She was aware that traditionally once a young women reaches her late teens, early twenties, she is expected to become engaged and marry. Although at first she thought "Are diamonds a girl's best friend?" trite, through writing and reflecting on her conceptual baggage she came to understand that, because of her own experience, she was really interested in discovering what young women thought about marriage and about themselves in relation to marriage.

> **Sarah:** I couldn't put it off any longer. I *had* to do this topic. I came up with a lot of reasons why I *should not,* but my writing was telling me that I couldn't afford to use this opportunity to research something else. I owed it to myself. Then, through writing my conceptual baggage around my research topic, lesbianism, I was able to find my research question, which became: "Why are explanations of lesbianism necessary and for whom?"

It took some time before Sarah felt safe enough to focus on lesbianism as her research topic. She kept changing her research focus. First she tried women's music, the next week her topic was looking at evaluative measures for grading. Finally, her writing helped her ignore the "shoulds" and claim her research needs.

SUMMARY AND CHECKPOINTS

Just to refresh your memory: researching from the margins is based on the commitment to advancing knowledge through a process of exploration grounded in the experience of people who have usually been treated as the objects of research. Both the tyranny of the expert and the mystification of research skills contribute to the public erasure and silencing of voices from the margins. We want to demystify research skills so they can be used to examine and publicly name how the experience of living in the margins affects our lives, our opportunities, the way we think and act. In this way we hope to explicate the social relations within which this experience occurs.

This chapter is the practical starting point for finding out how the mind of the researcher influences the research process and for finding just the right research question. The library tour is to practice observation, recording and reflecting skills and to describe the kind of *thought cloth* you weave. Combined with the ongoing conceptual baggage (Chapter One), you have now established a pattern of researching. The final step in Chapter Two is to refocus and refine the research question.

By this time, the overall conception of your research project should be emerging. As you move further along the research process, choices must be made about the appropriate techniques for data gathering and analysis and the presentation of the data. It is important to be as clear and concise as you can on the research topic before you progress much further.

CHAPTER THREE

Gearing Up for Data Gathering

---

getting ready
getting focussed
gearing up for data gathering ✔
planning for data gathering
gathering data
preparing for and doing analysis
presenting the data

INTRODUCTION

Methodology is the gathering of data and the making sense of it in an orderly way, as well as the study of methods. Methodology, theory and ideology are intertwined. How you go about doing your research is inextricably linked with how you see the world.

Researchers choose particular methods to unearth information not only because those methods permit them to get at the kind of information they think is important, but also because certain methods have been sanctioned by the status quo as the "proper" means of producing knowledge that will be recognized as legitimate. Because of this bias, certain methods have become well-developed while others have remained under-developed; certain information remains unresearched and undocumented. The methodology of researching from the margins seeks to address this imbalance.

The selection of the method is a critical aspect of researching and is usually based on what kind of information is sought, from whom and under what circumstances. It is important to recognize that methods appropriate for gathering abstract, theoretical information will not be equally appropriate for gathering subjective experience.

The methods appropriate for researching from the margins are grounded in a political awareness of the need for change. Information cannot be gathered without an understanding of the subsequent use of that information.

Similarly, information cannot be used without a critical understanding of the underlying assumptions. For example, one of the women who participated in Kate's research commented on the fact that you cannot use statistical data as though it were neutral. She said that: "For instance, implicit in the way census data is gathered is a set of assumptions that have to do with the state's attempt to manage a society in various ways. That is not to say you should toss them out, but you need to analyze the data with this critique in mind, knowing that you are looking at a particular way of classifying people for management purposes."

OVERVIEW OF THE METHODS: LOOKING AT OPTIONS FOR DATA GATHERING

The methodology of research from the margins is based on the commitment to advancing knowledge through research grounded in the experience of living on the margins. We do not want to contribute further to the public silencing of voices from the margins. Instead, we want to do research in a way that creates opportunities to reclaim and re-name that experience. We want methods that will enable people to identify and examine how living on the margins affects their lives, their opportunities, the way they think and act. In this way we can begin to focus on the social relations which daily help to construct that experience. In particular, methods from the margins must focus on describing reality from the perspective of those who have traditionally been excluded as producers of research.

Choosing a method for a piece of research is a political choice. When you choose a certain method you adopt a particular way of seeing and constructing the world which may prevent you from knowing it another way. Dorothy Smith suggests that the way professional knowledge is put together "... ensures that the bases of organization do not arise out of the discovery of personal troubles; it ensures that personal troubles become no more than public issues framed and contained within the public media, and that they do not become the bases of political organization uncontrolled by the institutional structures of state and relations of ruling" (1987:217). It is important to be aware, through all the different stages, of exactly how particular research choices organize the research process, the data and the analysis.

As researchers concerned about social change, it is essential that we consider how certain methods and ways of thinking may not only put limits on our questions or where we look for answers, but also may contribute to organizing the research process so that it remains a specialized activity rather than a resource available to all.

Part of what it means to live on the margins is that we are often required to perform a kind of doublethink / doublespeak in order to translate our experience into the concepts and language of the status quo. In an effort to comprehend and use the radical potential of researching from the margins, researchers need to maintain a focus on the world from the standpoint of the margins, to openly recognize the experience of marginalization and to use it as a touchstone. This involves an exploration of that part of what we know that usually gets left out when our experience is translated into the language of the status quo. We need to purposefully recognize and embrace the contradictions between "the actualities of our lives and the consciousness of the oppressor" (Lorde, 1984:114). From this vantage point there is a clearer and more authentic view of the centre.[1]

Methods from the margins are grounded in the following assumptions:

- Knowledge is socially constructed.
- Social interactions form the basis of social knowledge.
- Different people experience the world differently.
- Because they have different experience, people have different knowledge.
- Knowledge changes over time.
- Differences in power have resulted in the commodification of knowledge and a monopoly on knowledge production.

When one of the goals of the research enterprise is to challenge the monopoly certain groups have established on the production of knowledge, the need for methodology that encourages and supports this challenge is clear.

The five data gathering methods explored in this chapter are 1) interviews, 2) surveys, 3) participant observations, 4) life histories and 5) unobtrusive recordings. These are but a few of the ways that exist to gather information. To date these five are the most popular approaches among those researchers who have contributed to the development of this book. This section of the book focusses on data gathering methods which encourage the researcher's experience to be part of the content and the process of research.

---

1. The following quote, by Audre Lorde expands on the notion of clarity of vision from the margins. She writes that "traditionally, ... it is the members of oppressed groups who are expected to stretch out and bridge the gap between the actualities of our lives and the consciousness of our oppressor. For in order to survive [we] ... have always had to be watchers, to become familiar with the language and manners of the oppressor, even sometimes adopting them for some illusion of protection" (1984:114). For further reading on the voices from the margins, read bell hooks, *Feminist Theory: from margin to centre,* and Audre Lorde's *Sister Outsider.*

1. Method One: Interviews
Interviews are a special form of interaction between people, the purpose of which is to elicit information by asking questions. Definitions for interviews vary from "a face to face verbal interchange in which one person, the interviewer, attempts to elicit information or expressions of opinions, or belief, from another person or persons" (Maccoby and Maccoby, 1984: 499) to "a guided conversation whose goal is to elicit from the interviewee rich, detailed materials that can be used in qualitative analysis" (Lofland and Lofland, 1984:12).

It is preferable that the interviewer and the participant together define what form the interview will take. Oakley, for example, describes non-exploitive interviews as being situations in which the interviewer is "more than an instrument of data collection" (1981:48). The interviewer interacts with those whose lives are being researched, and records her / his own commentary; in traditional research models, the researcher would not normally be considered a source of information. In Oakley's approach, the interview is a discussion or guided conversation in which *both* the interviewer and the person being interviewed share information *and* contribute to the research process.

The essential components of an interactive interview are outlined in detail below.

(a) Formation and clarity of questions
The basis of all interviews is the question (Denzin, 1969:128). Your research focus must be transformed into specific questions with the help of your conceptual baggage and any preliminary information you have gathered in formal and informal ways. Among other things, this will help you, the researcher, stay close to the research focus, and will help the participant respond to questions about her or his own experience in an insightful and thoughtful way.

Where do the interview questions come from? From many sources. First, they come from your jottings. As you became interested in doing the research, you had questions to which you sought answers. Those questions are in your personal reflections, your **conceptual baggage**, and need simply be drawn out or highlighted. Second, questions come from what other people ask you or tell you when you verbalize what it is you are researching. Again, carefully recorded reflections about the research process will yield these gems. Third, questions will occur to you at odd moments – while you are dreaming about the research or while you are doing some mundane task totally unrelated to the research. Be prepared to jot them down, date them and later record them in your conceptual baggage. Fourth, if you have done some reading about the research focus, you will have some questions based on what you have read. All these questions, some of which will be raised by others, are of no more or less importance than any question you, yourself might raise from your own experience. *All* questions are potentially useful.

(b) Egalitarian setting and relationship between the interviewer and the participant

For quality interviewing, there must exist a sense of equality between the person gathering the information and the person whose knowledge is sought. Some combination of a set format with preformed questions and more interactive, spontaneously developed questioning is optimal. This creates space so the input of the research participants can help guide and shape the research interaction.

Many research descriptions address the problem of "researching down." When a researcher interviews participants that she / he considers to be less important than her / himself, the researcher is said to be "interviewing down." This suggests that researchers have greater authority in interviews than have other participants and that it is the responsibility of the researcher to attend to and minimalize this power differential. However, attempting to establish a "level playing field" for data gathering can also be difficult when a researcher is "interviewing up."

> **Kate**: Nothing had prepared me for some of the dynamics I encountered as a novice interviewing "experts." Although the class spent considerable time discussing ethics and the responsibility of minimizing the power differential that could exist between interviewers and interviewees, the assumption both in the class and in articles such as Anne Oakley's "Interviewing Women," was that the interviewer would be in a position of control. However, in my research, my control was not the problem. For example, two of the women asked for written statements about my research project when I first contacted them, indicating their professional understanding of how research is "properly done." Another woman wanted to know the interview questions before the interview. Partly from research inexperience and partly because of my experience in groups that negotiate the agenda, I gave her the interview guide. As she glanced over them, she told me they were the wrong questions. We finally managed to get over this initial "hump," and I turned the tape recorder on.

The need for equality in the research relationship does not mean that you and the research participants are the same. You may well share similar experiences, but *you* are facilitating a guided conversation which needs to be focussed on the experience you want to know more about. With that focus in mind, remember that you are responsible for "hearing the participant into speech" (Morton, quoted in Finson, 1985:103).

(c) Identification of your research approach to the research participant at first contact
It is only ethical that a researcher describe *why* the research is being done and *how* it is being conducted. It is important for the potential participant to be fully informed of the research focus and to accept (or reject) the invitation to participate.

(d) The interview is an instrument of data collection – but also a sharing of ideas and philosophy and experience and symbolic expressions ... a sharing of self
In an egalitarian arrangement, interviews are voluntary and either party may leave at will, preferably politely. Either the participant or the researcher can break off, withdraw, retreat for a time, ask questions, respond to questions, share or not share particular experiences.

In the case of interviews conducted by more than one participant, or more than one researcher, the nature of the data gathered alters because of the more "public" nature of the settings. The group dynamics differ from person-to-person contact and everyone in the group must agree on the way of proceeding.

The research participant is not a passive participant, simply there to talk about her or his experience. The participant may know of better or clearer questions to ask, of gaps in the interview plan and even of potential participants. If the interaction between researcher and participant allows for an optimal degree of sharing, both may reach new personal and political insights in relation to the research focus.

Intensive interviews seek to discover information about the experiences of the interviewee in the language and gesture of that person. Use the research participant's experience itself, as it is shared, as a guide through the interview. Where structured, standardized interviews seek to ask questions in a set vocabulary, in a uniform way, to participants for whom the context of the interview and the question pattern is controlled, intensive interviews are more likely to be guided by the need and intent of the participant.

(e) Recognition of the investment made by all: participants, researchers and others
Participants and researchers are involved in the data gathering. The following are illustrations of different interview scenarios. Each has different interpersonal dynamics.

— Two persons, interviewer who knows more about the participant than vice versa; they meet once and remain strangers.

— Two persons with somewhat similar experience who meet once. Interviewer guides the interview and records, the participant shares information.

— Two persons with somewhat similar experience, committed to the same movement (peace movement, women's movement, student rights, safety from violence), who have similar goals and may even know of each other. Both share information. The interviewer seeks permission to use information. Participant may see final research, be engaged in action at conclusion of research ... become involved. The interviewer and participant do not remain strangers.

— Two persons with similar experience, known to each other, who participate in the data gathering where asking back, an equal sharing of risk and of information is experienced. The interviewer and participant may at some time share political action or even reverse roles.

— Friend to friend.

— More than two persons.

The investment made by all participants is not equal, just as interest and personal goals for the research are not identical. However, it is essential to recognize that each participant and researcher is an autonomous human being with thoughts and feelings and experience.

Interviewing is not about meeting strangers, sharing information and then parting forever. If a degree of sharing about experiences has occurred in an interview, the participants are likely to meet again in non-research conditions. To presume that a researcher can "take the data and run" is inappropriate. So too is the whole notion of leaving a participant to deal with the aftermath of intensive interviews without being able to call upon the researcher in other than her / his research capacity. While counselling is not (necessarily) part of the research process, the scope of the research process must extend to cover the needs of the participant as well as the needs of the researcher and the research enterprise. For example, Hanmer and Saunders describe how, during their community-based study on violence against women, they found that the researchers were "sometimes afraid of 'blowing the woman's cover,' or further upsetting her, or of starting something the interviewer felt she might be unable to cope with" (1984:19). One of the actions they took in response to this problem was to organize regular group meetings for women who seemed to be experiencing difficulties with current or past violence. In addition, they always left information about how to contact the local women's shelter and rape crisis service.

The individual interviewed is most often a willing and cooperative participant who seeks to describe and explain, as best possible, her / his experiences and the meaning of those experiences as they relate to the research question. Good rapport between the interviewer and the individual being interviewed is fundamental to good interviewing. Some participants may even become collaborators to assist the researchers in making sense of the data gathered.

(f) Repeated interviews, longitudinal in nature, are often necessary to gather information about transitions or experiences that have been strongly felt

When the interview sequence covers repeated interviews with the same individual(s), the researcher will find that the need to build rapport and a firm level of mutual support becomes more evident. This is not to say that rapport and support are not also essential in one-time interviews, only that the need becomes more critical over time.

(g) Accounting for yourself as you research is essential

Potential research participants may accept or reject an invitation to participate in the research process on the basis of the researcher's identity and approach to the research topic. For example:

> **Lorene**: I knew I wanted to apply some of their knowledge, if appropriate, to my own quest for my sense of spirituality. I questioned whether or not this was like having a second agenda. I decided it wasn't because of the fact that I had explained to the women that I also was on a spiritual quest which was one of the main motives behind my research topic. I felt that type of sharing eliminated the idea of having had a second agenda.

> **Sarah**: Jane said she would not have agreed to talk with me if I had not been a lesbian. Her statement underscores the necessity for members of the community to be involved in the research, not only from the perspective of choosing the research focus, but also in terms of breaking through barriers to collect data. I suspect that none of the women would have talked with me about being lesbian if they did not identify me as lesbian. There is a nuance here which I am just now capturing. It seems that what is important is that the *interviewees* identify me as a researcher who is a member of the community. For me to say it is not enough; I must be accepted as such.

When Sandi researched Olympic athletes' retirement, she first made it clear that she was also an Olympian, who had a vested interest in the topic and an understanding deeper than that of a curious onlooker.

It is essential that all participants involved in interviews participate from an informed position ... cognizant of what the research is about and the destination of the information at the conclusion of the research project.

(h) It is essential that the interviewer and the participant both get what they want and need out of the research experience
Different interview situations call for different kinds of interaction between the researcher and the research participants. For example, the special needs of a willing but nervous participant, the dynamics of group interviews, or the outcome of a research collective or group of research participants disbanding before the research is completed must all be taken into consideration by the interviewer and must be accounted for in the research process.

The research participant may be unable or unwilling to explore painful memories if the interviewer cannot facilitate an appropriate environment for sharing. The interview is dependent on the skill of the researcher and the choices made by the participant. Both have the freedom to choose the kind of interaction in which they are willing to engage, and indeed whether they want to continue in a specific interview setting. The particular needs of all participants involved in the interview must be attended to.

Sometimes financial remuneration may be made to research participants, to researchers or to persons hired to assist with parts of the research. However, hiring individuals to be interviewed, conduct interviews or to transcribe and analyze interview material may bring an employer / employee relationship to the research experience. This would not be collaboration in the true sense of the word. When researching from the margins, it is particularly important to consider how the research may be influenced by funding obligations.[2] If persons are hired for particular tasks within the research enterprise, they must be fully integrated as collaborators and informed about the research, including their responsibilities in relation to other participants, the overall goals of the research and the particulars of each stage of the research, their involvement in gathering and managing the data and their participation *in the formation of new plans. Hanmer and Saunders (1984)* recommend that when money is available it be spread through a larger group rather than paid to one person. Because more people gain experience researching, there will be more people to take action after the results are known.

---

2. See Roxana Ng's *The Politics of Community Services,* 1988, a study which focusses on the issue of state funding in relation to community groups.

While traditional research methods have discouraged group interviews, feminists have argued that there is a need to shift the interview emphasis away from the isolated individual interview and towards repeated group interviews. They suggest that the "collectivization of women's experiences is not only a means of getting more and more diversified information, but it also helps women to overcome their structural isolation in their families and to understand that their individual sufferings have social causes" (Mies, 1983:128).

(i) The researchers must experience the interview as both an interviewer and a research participant early on in the data gathering process
Good interviewing is a skill. One of the ways to develop interview skills is to put yourself in the position of the interview participant, experience the questions as constructed by you, the researcher, and then reformulate the questions in light of the experience. To do this, have a friend or colleague who has some understanding of the content of the research interview you. It is particularly helpful, although not essential, if this person has some interviewing experience. This practice interview can mirror the circumstances in which you, the researcher, wish to conduct interviews with research participants. Record the interview in identical fashion to what is proposed for the research generally. Comments on the interview from your friend and you, the researcher / participant, then become part of the feedback on process in your conceptual baggage.

Since conceptual baggage is a major source of interview questions, the practice interview can be transcribed and placed directly into your conceptual baggage file. In this way, the content of the interview can be included as part of the research analysis. By experiencing an interview, you, the researcher, learn first hand about the process of being interviewed with the proposed research questions.

(j) The research process is a dynamic one, continually changing in response to new information and new participants
Researchers cannot interview everyone identified as a possible participant. Some people will be unwilling to participate, others will resist the development of any rapport and will therefore not be suitable as research participants. If there is a great deal of difficulty in finding willing participants, the problem may be with the research focus or the researcher. A good researcher will recognize this and adjust the research process or focus.

> **Sarah**: I don't try and talk them into it but I get the feeling they are balking because of the tape recorder. Were I to do this again I would make my initial approach in person so I would have the opportunity to discuss their fears and possibly set them at ease.

Every part of the research process teaches us a bit more about ourselves and the world. It isn't a matter of getting to the end at all costs. Rather, the way you get there, the process itself, is part of the research. Research is a constant process. Although a project may end, research never does.

Colleen: As you learn, you change and what you know then changes. As we change we create new ways of knowing.

The researcher and the research process will be changed at the other end, neither will be the same. Because it is a lived process, both are emergent throughout it.

(k) Collaborators are an essential component
Some research participants may want to share in the research process in a more involved way. They may want to see a copy of the interview guide before being interviewed, they may ask for a copy of the interview transcript or final analysis, or they may express an interest in collaborating on further data gathering or the analysis of the data.

Collaboration between a researcher and a non-researcher is useful. It offers at least two things: substantive feedback and personal support. Substantive feedback is that assistance others can give you which helps to clarify the content of your study. Personal support is just as essential and involves assistance others can give you which helps keep you clear thinking and motivated in your research. Both are equally important and, for personal support in particular, it is helpful if you can share information about the research process with someone who is biographically similar. If you have been physically battered in a relationship and are now volunteering in a job-entry program and researching the lives of women entering the paid workforce after a leave of absence, you may seek personal support from other women who have themselves recovered from physical battering.

Collaborative teams may be especially useful when large or intricate projects are undertaken. An example of a collaborative collective was the 1987-88 Organizational Review Committee of the National Action Committee on the Status of Women, a very large organization that lobbies the government on behalf of women. On a very limited budget, a committee of twelve women from across Canada met to guide and administer a massive survey of all N.A.C. member groups. While there were two paid consultants, there was a large committee that worked together to organize and complete the tasks. Here is how they worked.

A collective process was developed and in six months a mailed survey was created, distributed and analyzed; person-to-person interviews with fifty past executive members and friends of N.A.C. across the country were held; meetings were held in each region for information gathering purposes; a draft report was circulated to all researchers and participants, and after feedback a final report was drafted. Communication was constant, by mail and by telephone. All committee members consulted and were consulted on the central issues. The collective worked well to the deadlines and produced an excellent document exploring the way in which N.A.C. functions and lobbies for change.

Unity of purpose is one of the central organizing features of collaboration in teams. Trust and communication are also critical. In the above example, a national research project was completed by twelve people in a few months. An individual researcher would consider such a project as impossible.

In summary, the basis of all interviews is the question (Denzin, 1969:128). You must transform your research focus from one research question into many specific questions that will help you, the interviewer, stay close to the research focus and help the participant respond to questions about her or his own experience in an insightful and thoughtful way. The way in which you word the questions, the order in which you ask them and what the participant thinks you might be seeking are components of the interview process.

Different interviews follow different patterns. The pattern chosen should be related to the kind of questions asked and the nature of the information sought. For example, in the **intensive interview** the interviewer has a general understanding of the research topic and asks highly detailed, individualistic, exploratory questions that will vary somewhat with each research participant. In the **structured, standardized interview** the goal is "to elicit from the participant choices between alternative answers to preformed questions on a topic or situation" (Lofland and Lofland, 1984:12). Another goal might be to obtain, in a pre-ordered form, specific information from each participant. In this case a shopping list of "information required" is kept and the interviewer solicits information and fills in the gaps as best as possible during the interview. Regardless of the type of interview chosen, the researcher must pay attention to the components of good interviewing to maximize the encounter for both researcher and participant.

2. Method Two: Surveys

Surveys are widely used. They are "systematic collections of data ... through the use of the *interview* or the self-administered *questionnaire*" (Denzin, 1970:165). An interview guide (plan for interviewing) and / or the questionnaire are prepared before data gathering. To ensure that the best and most important questions are asked, we recommend that surveys be developed with and for the research participants involved. This not only adds a spontaneity and uniqueness to such surveys but keeps researchers close to the data and encourages close contact with research participants.

We suggest the following steps for surveying. First, the researcher formulates a research question. Second, with the input of other people who have a stake in the research topic, the researcher constructs questions for the survey. Then, a survey consisting of a questionnaire or an interview guide or some combination of the two is developed. The questions on the survey may be constructed so that they are closed (a limited number of choices) or open-ended (a question followed by room for comment and expansion by the participant). The researcher then identifies possible participants and begins to gather data.

For smaller surveys, information is usually collected at one specific point in time and analyzed soon afterwards. However, for large-scale surveys, many individuals may provide information at different points in time and in different contexts. These surveys are usually designed so that such differences do not affect the data.

Surveys may be conducted in person:

> *Well-founded Fear* documents how one research group used surveys in door-to-door interviews in one specific neighbourhood to study violence against women. They used personal contact not only to try to access information that may not have been shared without personal interaction, but also as an opportunity to pass on information about the local women's shelter. Having researchers personally involved in the data gathering was seen as being more likely to result in their continued involvement and action on the issue after the research was completed. (Hanmer and Saunders, 1984)

Surveys may be delivered and then picked up when they are completed. In cases where the time frame is restricted or the participants are in a local area, it is sometimes possible to administer the surveys in a slightly more personal manner. The following is an example of such a research plan.

> The task was to canvass the persons running in the November 1988 federal election on their attitudes toward women and women's concerns. In New Brunswick, candidates received a survey with questions. In the Fredericton area, the plan was that candidates receive a hand-delivered survey and an arrangement would be made for pick-up in the near future. The responses were to be used as information to assist with the preparation of an all-candidates meeting in several of the ridings.

As with interviewing, trained investigators may be employed to administer the surveys and to code and analyze the data. When researching from the margins, it is important that the researchers be intimately involved with the analysis and, if at all possible, with conducting the survey. **The more interactive the various steps in the research process are, the better the research will be.**

Not all selected individuals respond to surveys sent to them. Often, to increase the return rate to a level where statistical analysis becomes meaningful, researchers will make one or two follow-up contacts. Often the desired increase in returns results. However, there are exceptions.

> Shortly after the 1984 Olympic Games, a massive survey project was undertaken by researchers at a large Canadian university. The return rate was not as good as expected ... and the researchers did not know why. Follow-ups did not seem to alter the return rate. Personal contact with some of the athletes revealed that some were "questionnaired out" after the Olympics and were no longer willing participants.

Since the survey is in some ways a more formalized and less interactive process for data gathering than the interviews described in the previous section, it is useful for gathering information that does not require much social interaction.

3. Method Three: Participant Observation

Participant observation involves the researcher being a participant during the data gathering process. Participant observation combines ways of data gathering such as surveys, personal accounts / narratives, life histories / chronicles, unobtrusive measures (filming, recording), or document analysis with direct observation to give a full account of how individuals make sense of their experiences.

Users of the participant observation method make the assumption that it is possible to "stand in the shoes of another," to share and understand the intimate lives of others, if only temporarily. Direct participation and observation by the researcher is thought to provide meaning for the behaviours and attitudes expressed by individuals being researched.

There are several steps involved in the participant observation method:

1. focus selection
2. conceptual baggage
3. definition of the question
4. selection of site
5. initial contact on site
6. gathering (interviews, observations, participatory notes)

7. analysis
8. explanation
9. reporting
10. moving from research to action

Different degrees of involvement by the researcher are possible with this method: the researcher can be a participant; the researcher can be an observer; the researcher can be a participant observer. These options are described separately.

(a) Researcher as Participant
Participation involves direct contact with individuals and / or groups of people where they normally are and doing what they normally do. As a researcher, you might for example sit on a park bench and record the activity in a nearby area, talk with a person who sits on the bench for a short time, offer a bandaid to the young fellow who fell off the swing and teach one of the girls to do a forward roll when she asks. Information gathering can involve various degrees of participation.

The method of research from the margins allows for the fact that the researcher may be a long-standing participant. It is not only possible but likely that a participant who becomes a researcher will continue to be a participant after the particular research is completed.[3]

The degree of involvement by the researcher is something to be negotiated between the researcher, the participants and the setting or context of the observations. There may be anywhere from minimal to total involvement. Even with minimal involvement, the researcher's aim is to experience approximately what the actual participants experience. With total involvement, the researcher is immersed, if only temporarily, in the experience that is also being observed and attempts to understand it as completely as possible as a full participant.

> **Robbie:** As a member of the International Women's Day committee, my research was subjective. My involvement, my actions, my reactions, my feelings, my thoughts were very present throughout. I am part of the group. I affect the group's thinking, feeling, decisions, actions, as I am affected by it. I do not stand still, stand back and observe. I move along with the others. I change as the group changes. I change my ideas, my thoughts, my feelings, my actions.

---

3. When a researcher participates fully in an experience which is being researched, the usual textbook describes it as the researcher "going native." "Going native" implies a politic of **researchers** observing **natives**, a "we versus them" statement filled with hidden intentionality. In the enlightened age of post-racism, post-sexism, post-classism, post-homophobism, etc., such a term would never be used.

A note of caution: think through the potential consequences of being a full participant in your research process. In *Hookers, Rounders and Desk Clerks* (1982), the authors Prus and Irini describe how they participated as fully as possible without actually getting involved in the sex trade. Krieger (1983), author of *Mirror Dance,* participated fully in a women's community but had difficulty reporting on her research until after she had withdrawn from the community.

Being a participant provides an opportunity to develop greater felt meaning for the experience being researched. Some researchers choose to stimulate and sharpen their memory of the experiences that led them to their research question by seeking out related participation opportunities.

> **Colleen:** Yesterday I got out all my diaries I could find and have been wading my way through them. Now I am listening to records that go back to that time – Leonard Cohen and Joni Mitchell. I can picture locations, clothes, people, smells, feelings …

Through participation the researcher appropriates new information and new meaning. Even though perfect understanding is impossible, a measure of assurance about understanding can be gained from "standing in the shoes of another" and / or immersion in the setting of another. The sense of belonging, however temporary, gives the researcher some claim to status as an insider … with a brief measure of insider's knowledge.

It is essential that as a participant who is also a data gatherer, the researcher recognize the obligation to inform those in the setting about the research (i.e., what sort of research it is, for what purposes and who is involved). Research from a **covert** or **manipulative** perspective is not generally acceptable. The very basis of researching from the margins is honourable, overt relationships and direct communication.

This overt approach has been criticized for jeopardizing results. That is, people who know they are being observed behave as they think they should, (a phenomenon called the Hawthorne effect). However, in researching from the margins we think it essential that people be fully informed about the research that is done. Since we have altered the relationship between the researcher and participant, there are no subjects and subject deception is not possible (Reinharz, 1983:177). Further, if there is a real effort made to maintain an honest relationship between researcher and research participants, there is no need for "fake responses" (Klein, 1983:95). The participation of informed subjects ensures that research is done **with** and **for** the participants rather than **on** them.

Information gathered from a variety of sources will take its own shape and lead the researcher to make particular conclusions. Since there is no pre-established hypothesis to jeopardize, there is only information that leads to a variety of conclusions specific to the setting in which it has been gathered. The data will speak in its own voice.

Rather than concentrating on not letting the data deviate from a pre-planned pattern, researchers should use their energy to gather the information available and detail the intensity of the events and feelings and meanings in their field notes as they occur.

(b) Researcher as Observer:

Observers have an interactive relationship with those individuals being observed. On some level, there is communication taking place between those who observe and those who participate. Usually, though not always, an observer is a new person in the setting.

Direct observation of individuals and / or groups of people is likely to take place in the location where people are doing what they regularly do. Although the observer may feel outside the situation or interaction, that person's very presence involves at least a minimal level of participation.

It is important that the researcher's involvement remain **non-invasive** and **non-colonial**. Non-invasive means that the end does *not* justify the means. That is, while a researcher briefly shares the lives of participants, it is only as a respectful visitor. Researchers are in a temporary and privileged position. Non-colonial means that the researcher is likely to have a different way of doing things and of making sense of the experience. The researcher's way is no more or less correct than the ways of those being observed. A classic rule for observation is to not project your own meaning onto the experience of those being observed. Further, being non-colonial means that the researcher does not research to make life better for **the observed** by having them conform to her / his ways.

The researcher's record of the events is the **observations**; the researcher's thoughts about the events are **reflections**. These observations and reflections are often characterized by flexibility, spontaneity, open-mindedness (Dooley, 1984:268). As an observer the researcher has an opportunity to look and listen in a particularly attentive way and to study specific forms of communication and their meanings for individuals.

> **Brenda T.** observed women working as prostitutes on the streets of Halifax. She learned the language and its meanings; only then could she begin to record the essence of what she was observing.

As an observer, the researcher still becomes involved in the lives of the people being observed. How much and why depends on the researcher's sense of where the data may lie, her / his sense of responsibility to the individuals being observed, previous involvement and / or anticipated involvement with the same participants and ultimately the commitment to action as the research is brought to a close.

(c) Researcher as Participant-Observer

A combination of participation and observation is optimal. There are various levels of involvement from which to choose, depending on such things as the researcher's status as a participant (is the researcher a bonafide member?), skills and experience as a researcher, and level of energy and time the researcher is willing to invest. The possible levels of involvement are shown in this chart.

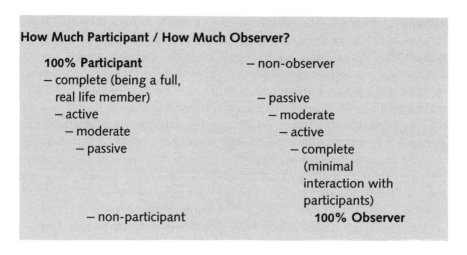

How Much Participant / How Much Observer?

100% Participant — non-observer
— complete (being a full,
  real life member) — passive
— active — moderate
— moderate — active
— passive — complete
  (minimal
  interaction with
  participants)
— non-participant **100% Observer**

Neither total immersion in activity nor non-interactive observation are likely to provide the quality of data available through a moderate measure of participation and observation.

Learning and sharing how others experience the social world is a difficult and often daunting task. Difficulties may include finding a place or position from which to participate and make observations, recording accurately so that little information is lost, finding ways to describe the masses of data, being ethical in the research process and making accurate descriptions in the research report.

As a researcher becomes familiar with the people involved in the experience being observed, enquiries can be made to those being observed about the relationship between what is observed (behaviours) and what the participants think about their behaviours (expressed attitudes and apparent meanings attached to them). Researchers are seekers, analyzers, and interpreters as well as data gatherers. Any events described and thoughts recorded by the researcher become **observations** and **reflections** respectively. All is part of the research data.

Just as the data is affected by the researcher, so will the researcher be affected by the data. As you, the researcher, engage in the process and interact with the data, the following is likely to occur:

- your consciousness about the research question will be raised;
- doing research will become action towards social change;
- the research process will be emergent over time.

In summary, participant observation, as a method, is flexible and allows for the combination of some survey methods (e.g., interviewing) with actual participation and direct observation by the researcher. The researcher uses what is meaningful and relevant, and incorporates personal impressions and reflections as part of the data. The researcher assumes the role of linch-pin between the data and the explanations of that data. The main drawback to this method is the sheer volume of data that can be collected and then must be analyzed.

Participant observation can result in an enormous amount of data. That data is specifically located and particular to contexts and biographies of the participants. The enormity of the participatory method means that new ways of analysis are needed for massive amounts of rich data, dense with descriptions. As one solution, Denzin suggests that a combination of methods can accurately reveal variety and meaning of observations.[4] Glaser and Strauss (1967) suggest the constant comparative method whereby observations are compared and relationships between observations can be seen. Both have considerable potential.

For all practical purposes, participant observation is a combination of several different methods: interviewing, surveying and documentary analysis (with extensive use of field notes).

4. Method Four: Life Histories

The life history method is a presentation of "the experiences and definitions held by one person, one group, or one organization as this person, group or organization interprets those experiences" (Denzin, 1970:220). Data for life histories can come from private documents such as diaries, letters or taped accounts, or from public records such as autobiographies, television or newspaper stories, minutes of meetings, doctors' records and the like.

In all cases, the usefulness of the life history method depends on the completeness of obtainable records, and the context in which the experiences and definitions occurred. The method consists of researching available accounts of certain experiences.

---

4. Denzin suggests that "no **single** method will ever meet the requirements of interaction theory. While participant observation permits the careful recording of situations and selves, it does not offer direct data on the wider spheres of influence acting on the self" (1970:26). He recommends that a combination of data gathering methods be used to examine a single research focus; this approach is referred to as triangulation.

The researcher's task is to bring the available data together to "make sense" of an individual's life. This is done by drawing as complete a picture as possible using an individual's own story. Then the comments of others who might have some perspective on the data are brought into the account. Such accounts are secondary to the original information. A description of the time and place the data comes from, as well as parallel historical events, is incorporated in order to give the personal story some context. The researcher must bring the different **bits** of information into relation with each other in order to fill in the picture. The following steps are used in the life history approach:

1. List the landmarks or milestones in the person's life.
2. Gather material by interviewing, library searches and so on.
3. Reconstruct the experiences of the individual by filling in a chronological account of his / her experiences.
4. Detail the reconstruction with information available from others and / or by incorporating parallel life histories.
5. Repeat steps 2-4 until, as much as possible, the life history takes shape as a relatively complete accounting of the individual's life experiences.

Life histories need not only address the lives of people who are dead. Present day life histories in the form of case studies can also be constructed. Interview transcripts, public accounts, private diaries, letters and the like can all be used to construct a case history of someone whose life is still unfolding. Biographies and autobiographies which rely primarily on first person accounts are good examples of this. Partial biographies, that is in-depth information about certain events or passages in an individual's life, can also be material for case studies. The strength of this method is that subjective data from many previously unexplored areas can be incorporated into what we know about the social world.

Researching from the margins includes doing our own life histories. Traditionally, experiences of those who live on the margins have been neglected and have thus gone unrecorded. In starting from experience, new possibilities for research using the life history approach emerge.

Because of the holes in our knowledge of the lives of those on the margins, room exists for misunderstandings, stereotypes and misrepresentations of who people on the margins are or have been.

What is known about the history of female athletes? These women climbed mountains in layered dresses, rode horses sidesaddle and even competed in swimming races while wearing corsets and hats. What do we know about the difference between the stereotype and the reality? The stereotype of the passive women comes more from the dress she was forced into than the nature of her desire for activity.

Some life history documentation about the lives of women in the 19th century would be welcome and could shed considerable light on the realities and the stereotypes of active women.

Life history research could for example be focussed on one individual's life, one individual's experiences related to a specific piece of their life, or even one's own life or a portion thereof.

> **Catherine:** When the topic is incest and it's your own experience, it is very difficult to pinpoint the time when you chose it as your research topic. By the time the course came along I was overripe. I not only wanted to do it. I needed to do it. I was longing for the structure the research process could give me to enable me to deal with this topic.

There is always interpretation involved in doing life histories. Although this is the researcher's role, it is not highlighted in the traditional descriptions of life history research. Instead, there is more concentration on documentation and less on the purpose or the perspective of the researcher doing the research. It is important that *who* is doing the research and *how* the interpretations are made receive equal billing in the final analysis of materials.

Generalizations are sometimes made from life history research. The room for pure conjecture is evident. Generalizations are difficult to make under any research circumstances and, if they are to be made at all, the researcher's focus and the original author's intentions in making records (diaries, letters, comments to the media, etc.) must have paramount consideration and place in the reporting.

Traditional life history researchers are encouraged to give priority to "testimony of schooled or experienced observers" (Denzin, 1970:247). Such testimony is considered superior to the untrained, casual researcher's view. However, the method of researching from the margins takes the opposite view. Too often our interests conflict with those of the schooled observer who has been trained in patterns of thinking that do not help us discover the information we need.

Life histories are heavily dependent on available documentation. It is necessary to ensure that available documentation is authentic and complete enough to begin a life history. If there are insufficient pieces of the puzzle, the resulting picture will be inaccurate and possibly misleading. Further, two researchers gathering information on the same individual may well write only vaguely similar accounts. The one that has remained closest to the available documentation, the primary data, will be the most accurate.

5. Method Five: Unobtrusive Measures

This method involves virtually all ways of recording in which the observer remains totally separate and non-interactive with those being investigated. Unobtrusive measures include physical trace analysis (e.g., where does the carpet wear thin in the house and what can be inferred from this about traffic patterns?), archival records analysis (e.g., number of immigrants from Nepal in successive ten year periods), non-interactive observations of a simple nature (body language, verbal language), time analysis (i.e., repeated observations at a set place and time) and hidden recording devices (e.g., tape recording or video recording of a social event) (Denzin, 1969).

There are a number of limitations in using unobtrusive measures for data gathering. First, as with a camera, the person doing the recording has a particular view or perspective, and this is what is recorded. Second, the recording is a snapshot view of the world; the researcher then analyzes the particular frame or record outside of its living context. This can lead to errors of interpretation. It can also lead to observing only those experiences which record well (e.g., fast action; high powered, dynamic people; colourful events, etc.).

Researchers from the margins usually critique the use of unobtrusive measures as being unethical. Present day examples of this are:

Peace marchers in Vancouver have registered their concern at being filmed by police while protesting at City Hall.

A woman was asked to participate in a videotaping about women in Canada. She later found that they used the record for another purpose without her permission.

However, there are ways in which we can use unobtrusive or non-intrusive methods without being unethical. For example, we may want to collect specific newspaper articles or government documents so we can examine how they describe the experience of being a "welfare" mother, or we may want to investigate how textbooks represent the history of Native people, Blacks or women.

In the process of chronicalling her experience as a member of the International Women's Day committee at Mount St. Vincent University, Robbie described how she randomly collected various public documents as they caught her eye.

Robbie: The newspaper clippings provided me with a picture of the social context in the university and the community at large. They gave me other opinions, thoughts and feelings beyond the immediate context of my research which were relevant to it and which further emphasized its relevance.

6. Summary

This section has addressed options for data gathering. Only five methods of particular interest to the authors have been included: interviews, surveys, participant observations, life histories and unobtrusive recordings. What these methods have in common is that they allow the researcher to engage in the research as a complete, thinking, curious and honourable person.[5]

PRACTICING / LEARNING RESEARCH SKILLS

This section consists of five practice exercises, one for each of the data gathering methods covered in the first part of this chapter. This is an opportunity to learn some new data gathering skills.

There are many ways to gather information. There are direct ways, among them interviews, surveys (interviews and questionnaires), participant observation, life histories and unobtrusive recordings. There are also indirect ways of gathering information: researchers may read reports, documents, books and other written sources to gain information without actually gathering data directly from individuals. A third, and often under-reported, source of information is yourself, that is, your own tHoughts and feelings, hunches and ideas about the research content. This is your conceptual baggage – the links between the emotional and the intellectual parts of you (Lofland and Lofland, 1984:10) that make the research process live. Some of these ways of gathering information have already been addressed in Chapter Two. Others have, at this point, been mentioned only peripherally.

To ensure that you use a method of data gathering that is both comfortable and appropriate, you should try on the method for "fit" to see if it is appropriate for your research focus and for yourself. The final choice of method must get at the information you require in a relatively direct way. A straightforward, simple approach is likely to be more satisfactory than an approach that is less direct and more complex. The route you choose has to fit you, you must be comfortable and secure in knowing how to gather data. Of course, developing skill takes time. So, rather than waste valuable time practicing your skills while you are actually conducting your research, we recommend that you "try on" some data gathering methods, as identified in the five practice tasks, to see which works best for you.

Five Practice Tasks:

The practices are meant to be fun and instructional at the same time. You can be as creative as you like as long as you are always aware that, as a

---

5. For further exploration of these methods, we suggest you read Denzin (1970), Glaser and Strauss (1967), Lofland and Lofland (1984), Johnson (1975), Roberts (1981) and Eichler (1980).

researcher, you have ethical responsiblities when your investigations involve human subjects. Your overall goal is to gather a small amount of data with each practice task in a helpful, understanding, safe and honourable manner. To help you develop data gathering skills, we have provided guides for the following:

TASK ONE: 15 Minute Interview
TASK TWO: A Sample Survey
TASK THREE: Two-Part Observation On-site
TASK FOUR: Small Section of a Life History
TASK FIVE: Unobtrusive Recording.

TASK ONE: 15 Minute Interview

This task consists of preparing and conducting an interview, transcribing the recording and summarizing how you have facilitated the entire data gathering process. This exercise will familiarize you with the complexities of interviewing. You can encounter problems in the practice task, deal with them and then be better prepared to anticipate and solve problems in a "real" data gathering excursion.

1. Research goals
   — to describe X (the research focus)
   — to explain X through the subjective interpretation provided by one individual

2. Sample research focus (choose one):
   — fears, as a woman (as a man), about growing older
   — decision-making about having a child
   — being the only (black / hearing impaired) in a group of (whites / hearing)
   — do we have political responsibility for what we know?
   — suicide as a way of dying
   — body, diets and politics

3. Conceptual baggage
   — what do I already know about X?
   — what do I want to find out about X?
   — are there any theoretical issues that guide this?

4. Who can I ask?
   — set up time and place (personal contact often works best)
   — recording method agreed
   — approximate length of the interview

5. Interview guide
- questions developed from conceptual baggage and from other sources
- questions ordered for comfortable interviewing sequence

6. Immediately prior to the interview
- pre-record on tape: identity (self and participant), date, time and place, topic
- set to record and pause
- paper and pen for jottings, copy of interview guide with you

7. Welcome participant
- introduce self and topic
- seek permission to tape
- turn tape on, record name and agreement to confidentiality
- explain how the participant can "go off the record" at any time by turning off the tape
- agree on approximate length of interview

8. Begin the data gathering
- set tone by talking about the two-way interview
- "Could you begin by telling me..."
- ask some of your other questions
- practice more in-depth questioning
- try asking questions out of order or forming them slightly differently than you had planned

9. Begin to wrap up the interview
- final question or two
- ask if there is anything the participant would like to add or ask?
- follow up steps (what you will do with the tape)
- thank you and shut off tape

10. Be attentive
- conversation after the tape is turned off is usually very rewarding and helpful to the research focus

11. Reflections
- make notes after interview: how you felt, interesting observations, recreate unrecorded patches for later use (but not quoting from)

12. Transcribe and make reflections in the margins.

13. Provide feedback to the research participant.

After doing the interview you will find yourself much more attentive to your own voice in asking the questions, to listening to responses, to engaging in focussed data gathering with optimal rapport.

TASK TWO: A Sample Survey

Surveys may include questionnaires or interviews or both. What is chosen depends on what you want to ask, how you want to ask it and where your participants are located. Some questionnaires can be completed on the spot in a relatively short period of time. Others are longer and more detailed and involve greater participant concentration. With this in mind, a researcher can arrange for a participant to complete a questionnaire in her or his presence, in a situation of the researcher's choosing or in a situation of the participant's choosing. Regardless, data gathering through questionnaires allows minimal personal interaction between the researcher and the participant.

Interviews, based on a variety of detailed questions, allow researchers to evaluate participants' accounts of their experience. Essentially, the researcher is a non-participant while conducting surveys.

1. Research question
   − answer the question "what is it that I want to find out about?"

2. Conceptual baggage
   − what do you think about the research topic and focus?
   − make rough notes about what you think, already know and / or have experienced
   − comb through these for possible questions to ask

3. Format questionnaire guide or survey
   − order the questions you have (e.g., from direct to indirect questions, from simple to complex questions, from public to more private and introspective questions)
   − are there other questions that you might want to ask?
   − do these questions really ask what you want to know?

4. Who can I ask?
   − organize a list of ten potential participants
   − contact participants to ask if they are willing to participate and give them a brief but direct account of the research question and research task
   − in the case of interviews, arrange a convenient meeting time and place
   − in the case of a questionnaire, arrange for the questionnaire to be delivered and returned (e.g., by mail, by hand)

5. Gathering the information
- conduct the interview by asking, one by one, the questions on your list. Add more if they seem appropriate. Ask the questions a little differently than how you have them written on the guide if you feel comfortable enough. Transcribe the interview if you have tape recorded it or write up your notes on the participant's responses to your questions as soon after the interview as you can.
- send out the questionnaires, collect them when they are completed

6. Analyzing the information
- how many participants answered your questions?
- how did the participants respond to each question?
- what other questions were asked or what other comments were made during the data gathering?
- are there other questions you would have liked to ask?

7. Summary
- what have I found out about the research question?

8. Feedback to participants
- write a short summary and distribute it to participants.

Some researchers conduct a small sample survey to determine what questions need to be asked and in what ways they can be asked most effectively. You may want to think of task two as a small but important part of a larger research project. The feedback to participants is essential. Participants have shared their experiences with you and expanded your understanding. Providing a summary allows for the exchange of information both ways. This is both ethical and essential.

TASK THREE: Observation On-site

Participant observation requires that you record, in an ongoing manner, the behaviours of the people you are observing. To do this, you could use a combination of, for example, interviews, surveys and some documentation. As an observer, you may or may not be a participant at the data site. As an introduction to field research, try the following:

1. Locate the data site: either an experience or a site which you think would be appropriate for observations. It should be something that is describable and safe for all concerned. Get permission if required or if you think it might be ethically wise.

Heather went to a laundromat every Sunday and decided to practice recording the "happenings" for two consecutive Sunday mornings. She was not looking for anything in particular, just a general understanding of who came in and did what.

2. Plan and participate in a two-part observation. That is, make two trips to the data site for a set period of time. Remember, who you are (or appear as) will have some impact on how those at the data site interact with you.

Heather made the two trips, once with her daughter and once alone. She recorded in an unobtrusive fashion who came in and what they did. Since she was a "regular" and often did school work while waiting for her laundry, no one paid her much attention.

3. Record as best you can what you are observing. You may also be able to describe what is not evident but might be expected to be evident. Further, record any interactions you experience and any on-site reflections about yourself as a researcher.

The long descriptive passages include what people wear to the laundromat, what time they arrive, with whom, some of the overheard snatches of conversation, their pattern in doing laundry and any comments they made about or to Heather.

4. In an ongoing way, record your reflections on what you are observing (why you think things are the way they appear) with the goal of building understanding.

Heather reflected on her own role as a Sunday morning regular and about being a focussed observer at a familiar site. She also commented on the unusual clothing people wear when they do laundry. She speculated that some simply wore whatever clothing they had left by Sunday and others seemed to wear "doing laundry clothes." The patterns of behaviour such as who regularly used what machines, how full they made them, what they did while the clothes were being cleaned etc. formed the basis for describing people's paths in the laundromat. Their conversation varied from plans for the trip to England next week to arranging for the children to get coffee and chips.

5. After the two data collection forays are over, describe what you have observed. You may then discuss the meaning of what you have observed, your role during the observations and how you might, upon reflection, alter the participant observation process.

Heather suggested that the same people arrived at approximately the same time and followed similar patterns during each of the observational periods. She also suggested that those who came in alone seemed to want little interaction and kept themselves occupied in a variety of ways. Heather thought that her routine was well integrated, that is, she fit in with the behaviour patterns of the others. Further, she recognized that as a participant she simply went about doing her laundry, but as an observer she remained on site after her laundry was finished, although she had no real reason for remaining. She also had to send her daughter off to do something else because of the distraction to the ongoing recording.

6. It is important to provide feedback to the research participants.

Heather was able to talk to very few of the people in the laundromat while she was making observations. Afterwards, when asked what she had been doing, she simply replied by describing her overall task and providing a sample of what she had been recording.

Participant observation takes a good deal of practice. One observer will record much differently and may become much more engaged in the activity than another. In situations where the participant observer becomes (or is) a full participant, extensive records of experiences and reflections will form a large proportion of the data.

TASK FOUR: Life History
A life history is a record of a person's (or group's) experiences from their perspective. The data sources for life histories can be personal accounts, private or public documents in which direct quotes are available and, if needed, third person accounts such as case-study records or biographies and the like. Since each person makes her or his own sense of the world, and that is the "stuff" of life histories, every effort should be made to give priority to the person's (or group's) own voice.

1. Select an individual and, after initial contact or after review of initial documents, select a portion of the individual's life to be described. Select a person and a part of their life or their work (e.g., a relationship or volunteer efforts) to examine in more detail.

Catherine attempted to chronicle her personal experiences as an incest survivor.

Errol examined the diaries of three women – a grandmother, mother and daughter from a farm community on Prince Edward Island.

2. Document, as much as possible, the personal view of the person on whom the research is focussed.

> Catherine went back to childhood journals and was dismayed to find only cryptic references to her experiences from the time she was 5 until she reached age 14. She recreated what she could, from year to year up to the present day.

> Errol identified segments of the diaries where the women talked about themselves or about each other.

3. Describe in detail and in an ordered fashion the selected aspect of this individual's life, as she or he makes sense of it.

> Catherine kept the language of the early journals intact in her data gathering. Later, Catherine reflected on the information contained in those early journals; she "layered the memories," adding subsequent impressions of her experience, changes in how she understood the experiences, displaying her anger, her forgiveness, her love. Both the information and the reflections are part of the data.

> In Errol's case, the instances where the women talked of themselves or of each other were uncommon but he was able to construct a probable character portrait of each of the women using her own words.

This topical life history is similar to a complete life history except that only one part of a person's experience is described. Several topical descriptions of the same individual might eventually be woven into a complete life history.

TASK FIVE: Unobtrusive Recording.

Unobtrusive recording is the way in which a researcher, though removed from the situation, gathers information about people's interactions or events in which they participate. The observations include surveys of public and / or private documents and recordings of events. Unobtrusive analysis is an approach to data gathering that limits the movements made by the researcher and therefore limits the impact of the researcher on what is being observed while it unfolds. The authors think it ethically indefensible to gather information about people's interactions without having permission to do so unless such information is on public record.

1. Think of a situation you could investigate without actually being a participant. Here are some examples:

 - physical traces left behind by people constructing a building, using a kitchen, writing on public bathroom walls

— archival records in the public library about who owned arcades in Edmonton prior to 1950, newspaper clippings about the athletic career of Diane Jones-Konihowski or early diary entries of Grandmother Rowe's trip from Saskatchewan to Nova Scotia in 1923

— recordings of peoples' interactions as they participate in events or do daily tasks: a gay pride march or performance of a skill (Debbie Brill's high jump technique or the aboriginal way of cooking a kangaroo in the Australian outback). These records are usually on film, video or audio tape.

2. Examine ways in which you can either record or gain access to records. Ask permission if it is appropriate to do so.

Amanda wanted to examine the breadth and depth of issues covered by Ann Rauhala, the women's beat reporter at the *Globe and Mail* newspaper. No permission was necessary as newspapers are public documents.

3. Examine a small portion of the material.

Amanda searched through each *Globe and Mail* edition between October 1986 and September 1987 looking for Ann Rauhala's byline.

4. What can be described and explained?

Amanda recorded the date, the title of the article, the page, the location on the page and the length of the article. From this data she made her conclusions.

5. Feedback to the research participants is the final step.

Amanda wrote a letter to Ann Rauhala explaining the project and enclosing a copy of her report. She invited Ann to comment.

This unobtrusive strategy is simple and straightforward. It can be much more complex, depending on the form of records used. For example, a more complex strategy might combine diaries, public documents and tape recordings about a single topic.

SUMMARY AND CHECKPOINTS

Researching from the margins challenges the assumption that all aspects of social life can be systematically and logically reduced to component parts of a whole. Further, research which is experientially based provides a richer data base with greater detail. This, in turn, leads to greater descriptive power in the resultant analysis (Glaser and Strauss, 1967).

The method of researching from the margins is part of a continuous process of learning how to create knowledge as the process is experienced. It is a dynamic and emergent process.

Checkpoints:

- Is the information you are interested in gathering of the abstract, theoretical variety or is it more of the experiential variety?
- What type of data gathering method is best for the kind of information you seek? What assumptions underlie this method?
- Does the method "fit" you and your research question?
- Are you aware of the political need for change in relation to your research focus?
- Could you combine two or three of the methods to gather information about your research question?
- Can you account for choosing one method or a combination of methods over others in a rational way?

CHAPTER FOUR

Planning for Data Gathering

---

getting ready
getting focussed
gearing up for data gathering
planning for data gathering ✔
gathering data
preparing for and doing analysis
presenting the analysis

PLANNING THE RESEARCH

People on the margins experience different social worlds than do those whose lives construct and define the status quo. However this does not mean that people on the margins share a common perspective. What people on the margins *do* have in common is the way ruling relations organize their exclusion, depriving them of "the means to participate in the construction of forms of thought that are adequate to express their own experience" (Spender, 1981:3). There are numerous examples. Women experience the social world in a different way than do men; marriage for a woman means different things than for a man. Blacks experience the social world in a different way than do whites. People with particular disabilities experience the social world differently than those without those disabilities. People with insufficient resources experience social life differently than those who have resources. Constructing explanations of the world is a human activity. And yet, knowledge production has been organized in a way that excludes many people from ever participating as either producers or subjects of knowledge (Spender, 1981).

1. We are all creators of knowledge.

There is a simple impulse in all of us to make sense of the world around us. As more complex questions are asked, new ways of finding information develop. Your search for "the sense of it all" through your research focus may occasionally get clouded and confused with "Am I capable enough?" "Research is the territory of experts" "What if nobody finds it interesting?" and "If I enjoy it this much, is it really research?" When you are beset by these questions and doubts, remember:

> If you can increase the understanding of an issue or a circumstance, illuminate one experience, portray one person's story in a new light, you will have helped others to understand the social world a little better. *This* is what research is all about.

To create knowledge requires that you be attentive to what you experience and to what others experience around you. In many ways, everyone does research daily in trying to account for why things happen as they do. Researchers go beyond the day-to-day descriptions and reach for more general, theoretical explanations.

Social research must, at a minimum, describe and explain what happens in the social world. Not all research is good research. As you are now aware, whenever something is written about your experience but does not seem to represent what *you* know to be true, both the knowledge and the research methodology need to be re-evaluated. So, too, as a researcher, if those you have gathered information from cannot see themselves in your reporting, then your research process and conclusions need to be re-evaluated. As a researcher from the margins, you are part of and a contributor to the environment of change that is transforming research methodologies.

Individuals on the margins have different knowledge, and that knowledge, as does all knowledge, changes over time. So, when you ask "Where can I find the information I seek?" you must first know the possible sources of knowledge.

2. Knowledge exists in many places
There is knowledge in common sense, not-so-common sense, tradition, authority and in research and writing. **Common sense** is how each of us interprets or makes sense of the world around us on a daily basis. Experience tells us that "it is so!" Everybody knows, for example, that drinking and driving are not a good combination of behaviours because innocent people can get hurt. **Not-so-common sense** is unreliable but nonetheless accepted knowledge. For example, many hotels are built without a thirteenth floor and the elevator counter dutifully records 11, 12, 14, 15 as it ascends. It is generally accepted in this culture that thirteen is an unlucky number. **Traditional knowledge** is based on our heritage. We learn, as we grow up in a particular culture, what is apparently true. An example of traditional knowledge for

many Canadians would be that there is a God and that God is a He. **Authority** is knowledge that we accept because we are informed of its existence by someone in authority. For example, we learn that vegetables are good for us because a parent tells us so. Knowledge can also be found in **research and writing**. Research provides us with the information, and conclusions based on that information, to support a particular research question. Research provides the reader with "proof" that particular knowledge exists. Writing commits to the printed page thoughts, words, ideas, stories and accounts all of which might eventually become part of public knowledge.

Researching from the margins involves four tasks. **Unmasking:** to question knowledge that currently exists, to understand who created that knowledge and why, what concepts and rules were used, and whose meanings or experiences are being presented. **Creating**: to build knowledge out of a basic understanding that social reality is constructed by members of society and that those on the margins and those within the status quo experience different social worlds. **Affirming**: to develop an understanding of the complex and subtle ways in which people on the margins are kept invisible and silenced; to affirm those on the margins by participating in naming that social reality in a way that remains faithful to that experience and does not further exploit it. **Sharing and reconstructing**: to act as responsible knowers; to use research skills to create knowledge for social change; to combine knowledge with action.

3. Who has the information?

Information comes from many sources but the primary source of information when researching from the margins is the people who have the experience you are seeking to understand. The way you gather the information will depend on your own experience, that is, your conceptual baggage and your training and instincts. Secondary sources of information – government documents, published works, private correspondence and other records – will also be of interest.

The primary source of information:
Researching from the margins entails gathering data about people in interaction with each other and finding out about how they understand their reality.

These individuals or members of groups may be complete unknowns or your closest friends and acquaintances. In determining who has the information you are looking for, remember that you are looking for information, not for representatives of a specific sample or population. As you focus on sources of information, you may know immediately who would be willing to be interviewed or where you might go for an initial participant observation. More than likely, however, you will have to start by asking others to help you locate sources of information. In fact, the more you talk about your project, the more you will find that virtually everyone has something to say to you about it. People may be referred to you, volunteer, or even provide you with lists of likely participants and helpful readings. But *you* must be the one who determines just who has the experience you are interested in investigating.

Among the criteria for identifying who might be appropriate for your research are:

experience: do they have the experience you are interested in investigating and how do you know that?

geographic location: are they accessible?

willingness: are they willing to share their experiences? is the information accessible?

contactability: can you locate them or can others identify them for you?

responsiveness: are they willing to participate? in successive steps?

identity: do they identify themselves as having the experience?

variety: do they have similar or different experiences?

communication: can you establish a comfortable rapport or atmosphere in which sharing of information can occur?

Some of these are self-explanatory. Identity and communication are expanded upon below.

Identity: In some instances, individuals or groups of individuals with the experience in which you are interested are clearly **identifiable**. For example, in Sandi's research about the female Olympians, there were only 134 Canadian female Olympians at the Montreal Olympics in 1976. The entire group (or population) was easily definable although quite difficult to locate in 1984 at the time of the data gathering. Robbie also had a very clear group to work with. She sought to document, through participant observation, how campus women organized for International Women's Day. She was already a participant in the International Women's Day committee and simply had to ask permission to record the events and individual interactions until March 8. Those involved readily agreed to her project and even offered to help her do some of the recording. In both enquiries, the entire population was known to the researcher before the data gathering had to be planned.

In other instances, it is difficult to **identify** those who have the experience you are focussing on. In both Sarah's and Lorene's research, participants were difficult to locate. Sarah found there were many lesbians with the experience she wanted to investigate, but very few were interested in sharing their stories in a "public" way. Fortunately, she was able to contact several women and, through a snowballing technique,[1] she soon had a short list of individuals who were willing to participate. Lorene started with two contacts and was led to a third. That was enough for her to gather stories about spirituality and get a toehold on what kind of research she was then ready to pursue. In both cases, these researchers relied on personal contacts to start the snowball rolling.

Communication: This is another criterion for selection of participants. First, since rapport is essential to good communication, it is important to be able to establish and sustain interpersonal harmony and understanding throughout all stages of the research. This means that whether you are gathering data or reporting on the research, rapport is important. Each step must take into consideration the effect on the research participants.

> **Lorene**: I've realized how significant the atmosphere of the interview can be; it is necessary to feel comfortable and safe in order for an interview to be a success. I met with Clyde, had lunch with her and talked for two hours before we actually began the interview because I felt we needed this time to get acquainted and feel comfortable with each other.

> **Tarel**: I had previously indicated that I would be bringing a tape recorder so when I arrived with it she was not taken by surprise. I also brought donuts so she would not feel inclined to be the host. During the time I set up the tape recorder we had been chatting and felt quite at ease with each other.

Good rapport can be fostered by complete and straightforward introductions of the research focus and of yourself as researcher. Any information that will ease participants' concerns is appreciated; this could include such details as confirmation of meeting dates and times, arrangements made for participation and feedback after initial encounters, and information about where the data will be used. Perhaps what is most essential is choosing a method that emphasizes "the ethic of *non-hierarchical relationships*" (Finson: 1985:112). Research from the margins requires **intersubjectivity**: an

---

1. This is a technique used to identify individuals who might be interested in participating in your research. Each person you survey or interview, for example, might be asked to identify another person who could be contacted. This process has worked well in work such as Brian Miller's *Indentity Conflict and Resolution: A Social Psychological Model of Gay Familymen's Adaptations* (1983), and Holly Devor's *Female to Male Transexuals* (Ph.D. dissertation in progress).

authentic dialogue between all participants in the research process in which each person is respected as an equally knowing subject. This does not imply that you and your participants are the same. Even though you may initiate the research interaction, the participants have the experience you want to know more about and their sharing will help shape the research. The researcher, the other participants and the research all change through the process. The communication between you should reflect the respect you hold for each other as individuals. You can help foster this by being as open and forthright as possible.

> **Lorene**: I offered them the choice of either writing down their experiences or having them verbally tell me their stories. I told them the actual research question before the interview in order to give them the chance to think and reflect on their experiences before being asked to verbalize it.

> **Brenda T.**: After the interview I asked the women what they thought of the questions and if there was anything else they would suggest.

When you are seeking information about sensitive, perhaps emotional topics, a safe and supportive environment is critical. This support may not end with the completion of the research. Researchers have often established long term friendships with people who have, at one time, participated in a data gathering effort. Rapport is *not* to be developed as a tool of manipulation to solicit more information from a participant. It is important to be open, honest and straightforward throughout the participant's involvement in the research.

There are circumstances where basic **communication** is difficult. You may be faced with a telephone interview or you may need to communicate with a participant who has a hearing impairment or who speaks a different language. In order to reach the best level of communication possible, full translation or mediated communication might be necessary. If you are not willing to have another person do the data gathering, or assist you while you do your own, you may lose important insights about your quest. Every attempt, within reason and available resources, must be made in order to ensure that **open communication** is established between you and the participants.

Safe **communication** is essential to good research. In some instances you, as a researcher, will be asked if you can guarantee safety to participants in your research. Safety is critical if you are gathering information that could stall or alter the course of events. You must communicate clearly your intentions to the research participants, particularly about the guarantee of anonymity and distribution of information at the completion of the inquiry. And you must adhere to what you have told the participants. Any changes require renegotiation with the participants. An example:

> Harriett was approached to participate in a video on women on the margins at a national conference held recently in Ottawa. The person who approached her said that the video was being made for use by faculty of a particular department of a university. Harriett agreed and participated in a 3 minute taped interview on being a visible lesbian in a national organization. She was surprised to find out immediately after the recording that the video was also going to be marketed nationally on educational channels. Weeks later, when the request for a signature of approval was received in the mail, Harriett did not sign it and wrote to the producer complaining of unethical treatment.

Harriett felt neither safe nor fairly treated and as a result the information she might have contributed was lost.

As a researcher you may gain access to information that could be potentially damaging to specific individuals, to groups or to political movements. In any exchange of information, researchers must guarantee that, to the best of their ability, they will adhere to the research plan and, if there is any deviation, particularly regarding the use of the information or actions undertaken, that the participants be informed and have the option to withdraw their participation. Researchers are responsible for establishing a safe, comfortable communication pattern so that participants can share what they are comfortable in sharing. If they feel "at risk," you must negotiate a different communication direction. If they do not want to share information, you must, after trying again perhaps, simply accept the stance they are taking and respect their choices.

When you ask "who has this experience?" you are beginning to focus on information, not on people. That is, you are sampling the information available to you, and should not be overly concerned about whether you have gathered the correct number of participants or a random sample or a complete population. Instead, if you think in terms of "how much information is enough?" you will soon recognize when you seem to have enough information for certain areas of your research but do not have enough in other areas. Keep that in mind as you seek to meet the criteria of experience, geographic location, willingness, contactability, responsiveness, identity, variety and communication.

Other sources of information:
Since your researching process includes exploring, describing, explaining and acting on a particular experience or range of experiences, *you* are integral to the investigation. The method of researching from the margins encourages

the integration of your own experience into the research process. Throughout your work you will find that your initial conceptual baggage (Chapter Two) and your ongoing reflections about both the content and process of the investigation (layerings) continue to be a source of information and analysis.

Documents can be a major source of information. However, much of what has been written and documented has not incorporated the voices or experience of those on the margins. All too often research documents don't speak to the actualities of our lives, even though they may claim to represent that experience. There are many "fine" pieces of research which are racist, sexist, homophobic, ethnocentric or classist. You might want to do an evaluative literature review or selected reading on the topics that have come up in the initial stages of your research. However, it is advisable to delay using them until the initial data gathering is complete and you have a better first-hand sense of how individuals with the specific experience make sense of that experience.

The production of knowledge from the margins is a radical enterprise. Its overall goal is to challenge the monopoly on the production of knowledge in order to transform the existing descriptions and explanations of social reality into an inclusive and truly human view and to contribute to making the social world a more equitable place for all. It is therefore essential to remain centred on the experience of individuals with direct experience, to include your personal experiences in the research enterprise and only then incorporate other documentation.

4. Where do I have to go to get the information?

The short answer to this question is that you must go to where the information is located or bring those with the information to you. That is not always easy to do. Lofland and Lofland recommend that potential data sites "need to be evaluated for **appropriateness**, for **access**, and for **ethics**" (1984: 13). Their work is the basis of the following discussion.

Appropriateness

Determining **appropriateness** means taking into account that *where* you gather data will influence *what* data you gather, what methods you can use and even what questions you might ask. Lofland and Lofland offer three 'principles' of appropriateness:

(a) If you choose participant observation, do your observations in a site where what you are interested in will be present.

(b) If you are interested in gathering information about some experience that doesn't occur in any specific site, more direct interaction through interviews or surveys is likely to be more useful.

(c) There are many varieties of the standard research methods and you may find that you have to adapt a particular method to suit your research needs; this may mean reconsideration of data sites in light of your novel approach to data gathering.

Although these points are based on common sense, and may seem obvious, they are important to remember when you are trying to decide where you will go for information. Many an extensive research project has gotten off track because of the inappropriateness of the data site.

Access

Evaluating for **access,** Lofland and Lofland's second point of assessment for data sites, involves the consideration of the setting, the researcher and the participants in the research activity.

The setting may be thought of as a place or a relationship in which data is gathered. As researcher, you may already be a regular participant in activities that happen at a certain place (e.g., a playing field, a school cafeteria, a political meeting room, a waiting room in a bus station, the transition house or at home). It only makes sense that your opportunities for research in the particular setting are likely to be different than those of a researcher who approaches the same setting as a stranger. Similarly, the setting may include a specific group of people. If you are a member of a group from whom you seek information, your access to them is different than an unfamiliar researcher's would be. Each approach has its own benefits and drawbacks.

As researcher, you are part of your own data site evaluation. That is, because of your ascribed and achieved characteristics, you may be more or less comfortable, have greater or less access, and be more or less successful in gathering information. There are certain settings which might not normally be accessed, for example, by a researcher of a particular sex or ethnicity or social class.

> Joyce Pettigrew, a young female anthropologist, sought to study Sikh rural factions in the building up of power of state level leaders. Both the role of women in that society and her kinship ties (she had married into a Jat family) made her participant observation research very different from what she originally intended. She had to gather information where she was allowed, first as a woman and only secondly as a researcher. In Pettigrew's research, her "personhood" affected how "intimately familiar" she could get with the rural Sikh factions. (in Roberts, 1981)

In a similar way to Pettigrew, a woman would only have access to a particular aspect of male prostitution. An anti-union researcher would provide a very different description of a strike action than would someone who was pro-union. A former alcoholic would provide a different account of a detoxification centre than would a non-drinking researcher. The point is not that these researchers avoid a study on these topics but that they bring their own characteristics to the study which may affect the data they can gather. These characteristics and viewpoints need to be identified and accounted for as part of choosing the data site.

Participants should have access to the research process; progress and focus should be as open as possible to participants. Since there are no hypotheses to prove and no experimental groups to influence, an overt and mutually interactive experience between the participant and the researcher is best. Participants need to know enough about the research focus to want to participate, be able to share in the information gathering process and, ultimately, to see themselves in the final report of the study. The researcher's key responsibility is to the participants.

In non-hierarchical, non-authoritarian, non-manipulative research, participants can easily be collaborators, helping the researchers locate other participants, interpreting the material gathered and assisting the researchers' access to various data sites (Reinhartz, 1983:181). Collaborators can not only provide data but can also participate fully in the formation of the research question, selection of data gathering methods, collaborate on the analysis and on the presentation of information.

Ethics
Lofland and Lofland's (1984:18) final point on access to data sites is about ethics. They ask two questions:

1. Should this particular group, setting, or question be studied by *anyone*?

When researching from the margins we are concerned with gathering information that will help us explore and transform current relations of inequality. We are less interested in pursuing research for the sake of research. Research which could contribute to maintaining or extending current relations of exploitation and domination should be viewed with utmost suspicion. Examples of such research are: eugenic engineering, mind control research, covert research on grassroots organizations, military research, research which supports or legitimates racist, sexist, homophobic, ethnocentric or classist actions or attitudes.

2. Should this group, setting, question be studied by *me*?

While researching from the margins encourages the use of your own experience as a starting point for research in order to acquire rich, dense data, it should not be thought that you must be a rape victim to study rape victims or be a New Democrat to study New Democrats. However, it is the rare researcher who can do full justice to a research question if there is *no* experiential basis from which to begin.

While, as Lofland and Lofland suggest, researchers can sometimes "transcend ethnic and cultural differences" (1984:17), researching from the margins is best accomplished by those who live on the margins. The simple reason is that, in speaking from the margins, convincing testimony comes best from those who live it. Also, because they experience the world differently they have a better sense of what research questions need to be addressed.

A possible exception to this might be if the researcher were to collaborate with those close to the experience throughout the research, taking direction for the focus and questions from them and clearly identifying her/his experiential self at the beginning of the research.

> I am a white, middle class university-educated male. I have been studying the experiences of men who are living and working in much poorer economic circumstances. I am interested in listening to their voices and in the research have given those voices priority. The men have defined the focus of this project, named the important questions and participated in the analysis that is being presented.

Or research may be undertaken in order to get a better understanding of the felt experience of a particular group. For example, Neil carried out a seven-day simulation of severe bilateral hearing impairment. He hoped that by experiencing the world in this way he would gain a better understanding of what it is like to have a hearing impairment in a hearing world. He hoped this experience would help him be a better teacher.

> **Neil**: When I was involved in a conversation or a situation with someone who was doing a lot of talking, I often had a great deal of difficulty understanding it. If after asking for clarification several times I still did not fully understand, I would pretend I did and end the conversation as quickly as possible. What made this strategy viable was the fact that many people were willing to believe that I understood. This is something that teachers need to keep in mind when explaining things to their students.

Because knowledge is socially constructed, it can be used to validate and perpetuate or challenge and change the power and authority of certain groups. For this reason we think it politically unwise for those whose interests parallel those of the status quo to research those on the margins.

Social interaction is at the root of all social knowledge. Therefore, it makes sense that information is gathered about social interactions. Given that knowledge changes over time, the process used to discover knowledge needs to be equally dynamic and adaptable to change. The methodology of researching from the margins recognizes, indeed stresses, both these points.

SETTING THE STAGE

This section of the chapter is about choosing a data gathering approach. This is an important moment in the research process where you begin to make a commitment to some specific method of inquiry. You must decide for yourself what kind of data gathering you want to do, who you want the participants to be, how much time you have to do the research, how you will go about recording the information and who can help you with various tasks and considerations.

There are five steps to finding the data gathering approach best suited to your purposes.

First, write out your research question.

Nothing you might want to research is too small or insignificant to be of value to yourself or those around you. What is interesting to you, problematic for you or of immediate concern to you is worth researching. For example:

> Judie chose to research "speaking from the edge" because of her experience of trying to communicate in two very different social worlds, one academic and feminist and the other non-academic and non-feminist. She understood at the start that the project would not change the lives of many people but that it would have some impact on her life and the lives of those around her.

The whole research enterprise is dependent upon you, the researcher, and it is important that you keep close to what is significant to you, that it "feel right." If you are curious, excited by what happens around you, questioning, excited about learning, disciplined, anxious about getting research done right, passionate, angry or tenacious you will be a good researcher. If you are complacent or insincere, your work will fail to meet the criteria of good research because it will ring false to those who have the experience you are trying to describe and explain.

Second, ask yourself the following three questions.

1. What do I expect to find?
   – specific information
   – more questions
   – answers

Regardless of your response to this first question, it is important that you understand and record your expectations for the research process (conceptual baggage).

2. What benefits do I expect to gain?
  − make the world a better place
  − get an answer to a nagging question
  − learn about the research process

Again, it is less important to come up with a specific response than it is to consider the question itself.

3. What effect will this have on the lives of those from whom I gather information? [2]
This is an important question to keep in mind throughout the research enterprise. As the researcher, you will become a more informed person and this means you will carry the additional responsibility of that knowledge. Your research participants will also become more informed and will share that burden of new knowledge. Be aware that new knowledge is not always easy to bear and can sometimes lead to major changes in the lives of both researchers and collaborators.

4. What responsibilities do I have to others and how might they shape the research?
Things you might consider are: Who pays the bill for this research? Is there a link between myself and the funding agency? How does that affect or shape the research enterprise? Even without funding, the research may be shaped differently depending on your obligations to academic or other institutions, to grassroots groups or to political parties.

Third, select the data gathering method that best gets at what it is you want to research.

The choices of research method presented in this book are interviews, surveys, participant observation, life histories and unobtrusive measures. Be creative − combine, alter and adjust. The development of the method will depend on your input. As in the library tour, follow your instincts; make sure you record the steps you take and account for them carefully. Choose what fits you and your research question best. Here are two examples:

---

2. In addition, you might also ask what expectations do others have about your research and what benefits are expected.

> I will recount the observations, describe the structures and suggest a critique for the downward spiral of homelessness. (Harman, 1989)

Harman chose to examine the lives of homeless women in a large urban centre in Canada. She decided to describe and analyze the social structure in the homeless subculture and develop the critique. In the end, she also gave an impassioned description of the women whose lives she touched.

> The particular meaning and significance of the guiding idea, that the analysis of talk between patients and physicians is a primary source for understanding clinical work, will be developed and specified in the reporting of methods, findings and interpretation of data. (Mishler, 1984:5)

This introduction explains that the intention of the research is to improve the data gathering potential of interviews between patients and physicians. The data gathering is a careful examination of the ability of current procedures to gather information that is diagnostically important.

Fourth, form your questions.

At this point, you must begin to develop more questions: ones to ask in an interview or on a survey, ones to keep you anchored or focussed as you pour over documents or observe people on the street. The questions you develop here will come almost completely from the conceptual baggage you have been keeping (see Chapter Two). Here are some examples:

> **Flo**: I formed questions that I hoped would stimulate the participants to share with me their feelings about how they worked through the process to arrive at their decision to return to university and how they now felt about that decision.

> **Tarel**: I formed my questions from the recurring themes in my conceptual baggage.

> **Kate**: Returning to university, I was acutely aware of the real limitations of the form, language and subject matter which are required from a student / academic in order to be taken seriously. Questions which focussed on the relationship between feminist research and the feminist community came out of this experience.

Fifth, find a shoebox.

You already have a file folder or notebook containing your conceptual baggage. You now need a place to keep all the bits of information about *why* you are choosing a particular method, *what* you expect to learn from the enterprise and other information you will begin to collect – jottings on napkins or pieces of paper, newspaper clippings, an article on your topic passed along by a friend. It is important not to lose bits of information just because there might not be a ready place for them. For these, it's a good idea to have a box or a drawer reserved for collecting such information. A shoe box is just the right size for smaller projects. Simply date each piece of information as you put it in the file. When the time comes to account for why you constructed the research process as you did, the helpful information will be in a box waiting to be chronologically ordered for the final account.

Make careful and regular notes on both the content (what you find, why you choose a particular method, your expectations and reflections on those) and the process (how the research process is actually organized and your reflections on the process) as you experience it. List helpful hints and reminders where you can see them frequently. Leave yourself lots of room for reflections and layering in different coloured pens. Leave half of the page blank for comments, reflections and further layering over time on any ideas and information gathered. The more you gather information, the more these files will be used and become familiar to you. This is the beginning of **living with the data**. Now you are almost ready to begin gathering your information. But, there is one last step.

Sixth, planning your time and resources.

An essential organizing tool is a timetable or grid of the territory to be covered by the research. This could take the form of a chart or a rough sketch of information that could contain things such as who might have information that you are seeking and where they are located, how much time you might need for gathering information and making sense out of it and, finally, when you anticipate finishing the research.

This grid is only a set of signposts, a checklist to ensure that you stay on track. But it can help you see the entire picture when you have been working intensely on one small aspect of the work. Later on in the research process, if you feel overwhelmed by the sheer volume of information you have collected and you begin to think that you will never do justice to the voices you have heard, look back to the grid to see how far you have come in the process and think about how much more you understand now than you did at the start. It's a great motivator!

Prepare a list of the skills and resources available to you during the course of the research. For example, what research tool is preferred? What personal attributes do you bring (e.g., tenacity, logic, order, creativity, inspiration, education, experience, thoughtfulness, reflection, working ability, insight, flexibility, dedication to the task)? These are important because they determine, to a large degree, how you will approach the data gathering and analysis. You, the researcher, are integral to the research process and the results.

SUMMARY AND CHECKPOINTS

To be a researcher, you have to think of youself as having the potential to create knowledge. Information is everywhere and you must learn to be attentive to the information that will help you achieve greater understanding. Being a researcher also means that you become disciplined and learn to account for how and why you gather information and how you make sense of it.

Information comes from many sources, but in the method of researching from the margins, priority is given to the information that is gathered directly from people who have the experience researchers are interested in knowing more about. Secondary data is important but does not overtake the experiential data during the research process. Despite the weight of authority of some documents, we believe that they should not be referred to until after the initial analysis of the data has occured. In that way, the researcher can be open to new questions and new ways of asking familiar questions.

To maximize the potential for gathering data, researchers are encouraged to carefully plan the data gathering forays. This includes planning the data gathering settings, informing the prospective participants, organizing the appropriate recoding methods and readying yourself to be a data gatherer.

Checkpoints

The data gathering approach you choose must enable you to research peoples' lives, their experience and the meaning their experience holds for them.

- Is my research grounded in the experience of the participants?
- Have I reflected on the data gathering process? Have I prepared for ongoing reflections as I begin to gather data?
- What is the best way(s) for me to record new data?
- Do I account for myself in the planning of the research?
- Do the potential participants have the experience I want to know more about?
- Is the research site optimal?
- Is my grid (timetable) realistic and have I accounted for those other activities which might take me off track?

CHAPTER FIVE

Gathering Data

---

getting ready
getting focussed
gearing up for data gathering
planning for data gathering
gathering data ✔
preparing for and doing analysis
presenting the analysis

INTRODUCTION

Gathering data is the central part of any research process. It is the collecting of information and reflecting on the meaning of that information that provides new insights into how the world is understood. For researchers on the margins, this means using familiar methods in new ways, asking old questions in new ways and asking new questions. It may mean gathering information from people who want to know what you will do with the information before they will share their understanding of their experience with you.

Researching is about gathering data. This phase of the process consists of meeting with the identified research participants, going through your questions with them and / or making your observations and recording the information. This may be the most exciting stage of the process because you are gathering so much information that will enable you to answer your research question. You are well on your way to saying "I have figured it out!"

STAGES OF DATA GATHERING

Before contacting prospective participants, you must work out precisely how you want to describe your research project, what you would like from the participants, what you can provide for them and what you anticipate you will be doing with the information afterwards. Ask yourself the following questions:

- How am I going to introduce my research project?
- What am I measuring and describing?
- How am I measuring and describing?
- What are my recording methods?
- Do I need someone else to assist me in making contacts (gaining entry)?
- Who is involved (collaborators, participants, sponsors)?
- Do I have clear plans for analysis and destination of the research information?
- Is this the right research method for this research question?
- What assurances can I provide to the participants about the use of the information they provide and their place in the reporting?
- Can I be myself in the research process?
- Do I have permission from the necessary ethics review board if needed?

Checklist (before contacting participants):

for interviews

- Are the questions clear in my mind?
- Do I have an interview guide ready?
- How do I want to contact the participants: by telephone, by mail or in person?
- How long will an interview take?
- What kind of interview setting is most appropriate?
- How much do I want to say in that first contact?
- What kind of anonymity can I guarantee?
- What times do I have available for interviews and for reflections afterwards?
- Do I want participants to prepare in some way, to think about the topic beforehand or to bring some documentation?
- What if they decline?
- Others

for participant observation

- Is my role clear to me (degree of participation / observation)?
- Is the research focus clear?
- Am I fully prepared to gather information (prepared to go into the field, recording procedures clear, possible questions formulated)?

- How long do I plan to stay in the field?
- Do I have contingency plans so that I can gather information when and where it appears?
- Can I record my observations accurately? Is my grasp of the language and my understanding of the meanings clear enough to gather information accurately?
- Am I doing the research for the right reasons, in the right place?
- Others

for surveys

- Is the survey designed and ready to distribute?
- Is there a hidden agenda to the research? If so, how can I explain it better so that it is overt, not covert?
- Is there an introductory letter explaining the important aspects of the research project (what, where, when, why and how)?
- If mailed, do I have the complete, most recent addresses? Is there a stamped, return envelope included? Do potential participants have enough information to complete the questionnaire? Is there a follow-up procedure in place to ensure that people are reminded to return questionnaires as soon as possible?
- If the survey is conducted in person or by telephone, do participants have room to decline to respond to some or all of the questions?
- Is there a follow-up procedure in place so that people can be informed about the research results?
- Others

for life histories

- Do I have permission from the person to be researched, their immediate caregivers or supervisors, or their estate?
- How much information is needed?
- What kind of information do I *not* want?
- What kind of information will I give priority to?
- Who can be helped or hindered by this information?
- Who might need to review it before it becomes a public document?
- Is there someone I might collaborate with?
- Others

for unobtrusive recording

- What kind of content am I looking for and why?
- Where am I likely to get it?
- Am I familiar with the recording equipment and can I cope with any minor equipment problems?
- Do I have permission from the participants or are the documents I need publicly accessible?
- Does what I gather relate to what I want to know?
- Do I need to illustrate the information?
- How can I ensure that I understand correctly?
- Are there political or legal barriers to this research?
- Others

Once you are fully prepared, you are ready to contact potential participants and / or get access to the documents you need.

1. Making contacts

In Chapter Four, you developed the basic research design consisting of a grid (timetable) and the method by which you intend to gather information for your research. Now, your intention to do research is ready to be translated into action.

There are many types of contacts to be made. You must contact potential participants, gain access to documentary discourse (documents, diaries and the like) (Smith, 1984) or negotiate access to particular settings.

(a) Contact with potential participants and documentary discourse:
As Lofland and Lofland (1984) indicate, making contact is not always as easy as it may seem. They write that "it is one thing to decide for yourself about interest, appropriateness, accessibility and ethics; it is quite another to get all interested parties to go along with your plan" (1984:20). Your contact may be directly with those who have the experience you are researching, as in the case of interviews, surveys and participant observation. Or your contact may be indirect, where your main concern is with documents, diaries, letters and the like. In any case, the following concerns are of paramount importance to doing good research:

- you act honourably (see Glossary)
- in situations where information is gathered directly, recognize that participants
  - are your equals
  - are autonomous

are unique

decide what they want to disclose to you

have the right to decide what gets recorded

are sources of information and must construct their own
meanings about being research participants.

— participants are neither passive nor subordinate, and both
participant and researcher have relevance and significance to the
research project (Mishler, 1984).

— you are researching how participants view their experience and
the experience of others. It is not acceptable to ask how they
think someone else thinks about something, nor to correct their
version of particular events with your version of events. What is
important is *their* perception of *their* experience.

The aim of your research is to describe and explain your research focus
through the subjective interpretations provided by people's own definitions
and explanations of such experience.

Potential participants can be contacted in a number of ways. The usual
approaches are through personal contact, telephone contact or by mail.
Occasionally, contact can be made through a third person who might introduce the research to the potential participant and then, if it is agreed, introduce the researcher to participant. Provided here are examples of making
contact for the purpose of interviewing and for surveying.

Interviews
A first contact will go something like this:

— introduction of self and research focus
— time and place of interview
— description of interview setting
— description of proposed recording methods
— length of time needed for the interview
— particular note of any sensitive material
— describe any preparation needed
— arrangements for confirmation or alteration in plans

Here is how some researchers reported their first contact with a potential
interview participant.

Tarel: The participants were first approached at the university or at
their homes and asked if they would share their experiences with
me.... Then I contacted them by phone to set up a convenient time.
All the participants were interviewed in their own homes since my

own home is inadequate for entertaining and I was not interested in carrying out an interview in a public place because of the impersonal atmosphere.

Heather: D. was my first participant. I made contact with her on Thursday, the 19th at 5:20 p.m. She was very receptive and agreed to an interview. I informed her that I would get back to her about the particular time and place. I then phoned C. at home at 8:10 p.m. I was determined to make sure I had everything right so I sat down beforehand and prepared a short introduction. When she came to the telephone, I was ready. I finished my little speech without interruption and she asked me to repeat my name and then asked when I would like to do the interview. She agreed to March 3 at her place of work. She instructed me to go to the lobby of the building and from there, someone would show me up to her office. She was polite and very friendly. She made me feel very much at ease.

Sarah: I don't try to talk them into the interview but I get the feeling they are balking because of the tape recorder. Were I to do this again, I would make my initial approach in person so I would have the opportunity to discuss their fears and possibly set them at ease. The woman I spoke with on the phone was willing to become involved and it was the person I didn't talk with (the partner in the lesbian relationship) who decided otherwise. They both cancelled. Next time I'll talk personally with each.

Lorene: I spoke with each woman briefly about the topic of spirituality to see how it felt talking with them. Intuition on my part played a significant role in choosing the women I wanted to interview.

In each case, the participants were contacted well before the interviews actually occurred. This allowed participants to think about the topic and about being interviewed before the event. In most cases, the contacts were successful in providing an interview participant. In Sarah's situation, she received permission from one partner in the couple and subsequently received a call to cancel the interview. This has as much to do with the research focus (lesbian identity) as with Sarah's approach. It is important to get permission from each fully informed participant before arranging the interview time and place.

Survey
First contact with potential survey recipients consists of the same elements of information as the contact with the interview participants. If a questionnaire

is to be used, a cover letter explaining the research focus and introducing the researcher is often delivered simultaneously. An introductory letter that is sent out ahead of time can set up an anticipation and / or preparation that can be beneficial.

The elements such a letter includes are: the identity of the sender, purpose of the research, the reason for the recipient's selection, guarantee of anonymity, length of time required to complete the questionnaire, deadline for completion, instructions about the completed questionnaire, request for an indication of willingness to be further involved and notice of where the results are to be discussed, published or posted.

Here is an example of a cover letter.

Date

Dear ———

   We are a small group of volunteers from the sexual assault centre; we're meeting to discuss ways to make volunteering more satisfactory. We are at this time trying to understand why there is considerable turnover among volunteers who work evening shifts. As someone who has experience being a volunteer at the centre, we ask you to fill out the attached questionnaire. All questionnaire information will be kept absolutely confidential. The questionnaire is part of a small survey.

   Only those who have volunteered in the past two years for more than ten hours per month are being asked to respond. You are one of only 37 who meet this criterion.

   The survey should take about one half-hour to complete. Please take the time to do so and return it to us in the stamped, return addressed envelope by June 30. We will be contacting a number of the volunteers for more in-depth interviews. If you would like to be interviewed, please indicate that on the front page of the questionnaire in the place provided and include a telephone number where you can be reached.

   The results will be discussed by the volunteer collective, printed in the monthly bulletin and posted on the notice board. We hope to take the concerns and organize around them to bring about change.

   Thank you.

   Sincerely,

Letters of introduction or permission may also be needed to gain access to certain documents, diaries and letters. Such introductory letters should contain similar information.

(b) Contact to gain access to settings:

Since access will influence how the research is defined by the participants and what information can be gathered, each research project will have its own access dynamics. In some instances, researchers need assistance to gain access to some settings. If observations are to be made where a different language is in use, where special access permission is needed (e.g., union strategy meeting or government nuclear shelter) and where assistance with gathering and description is needed, researchers can invite individual collaborators to assist with the access experiences. Collaborators might, for example, be asked to make connections and assist in direct introductions to people in these settings.

Access can be gained by request, by invitation or by happenstance. The access is generally granted by either the participants as a group or by individuals. Depending on the research focus, permission from authorities may also be needed. In rare instances, a researcher has been known to exchange some service for the privilege of observing in a particular setting.

For example:

> **Brenda T.**: I worked as a volunteer at the centre until I had gained enough of the prostitutes' confidence so they would take me out on the street. Individuals explained the language and the meaning of different transactions so that I could understand what was happening on the street. Later I went to the homes of the prostitutes and found I had much in common with them.

In this example, the researcher needed a helping hand to gain access. The women on the street were participants and, at the same time, collaborators. After a while, the researcher developed a bond of friendship with the participants and subsequently worked as a volunteer lobbyist on their behalf. Brenda was always forthright, expressing her interest and need for collaboration. At no point was manipulation involved.

* Anonymity

Often potential participants will want a commitment from you to guarantee their anonymity. It can be of crucial importance to people who live their lives on the margins of the status quo. The researcher must know and be clear about what can be guaranteed and what cannot. If you want to guarantee anonymity to your participants, you must know precisely how that is done. Anonymity means that readers of the research will be unable to identify participants by name, through the experiences being described or by location.

Lofland and Lofland (1984) point out that anonymity is only a matter of degree. In the method of researching that is being discussed in this book, it is imperative that the voices of the participants come through in the writing and that the individuals be able to identify their own quotes. However, this does not mean that anonymity is non-existent. It simply means that participants must be able to see themselves and their experience in the research reports. At the same time, every attempt can be made to ensure that no other participant or reader of the research will be able to identify the participants.

There are a number of ways to alter data to increase the degree of anonymity. First, when the data is being recorded, determine who else might have access to it. If data management arrangements will require one or two others to see the raw data, you must ensure that participants agree. For example, if someone other than the researcher transcribes the tapes, you must get permission from the participant. If you plan to collaborate with others during the analysis, to more fully understand the context or meaning of information, the research participants must agree in advance. Second, when the data is ready for reporting, the researcher must ensure that the participant is not identifiable. Names and places can be changed, places of work or types of work, age and sex can be altered. Names can be left out entirely and different initials can be used instead. Researchers may alter some or all of the situation, experience, personal identity and time frame in an effort to provide anonymity with minimal change to the context and meaning of the participant's experience.

2. Beginning to gather data

The plan for data gathering that you have developed (Chapter Four) can now be put into effect. The process of gathering data through interviews, surveys, participant observation, life histories or unobtrusive observation (or some combination thereof) will be a dynamic experience. Just as the process settles into a pattern, a new problem will arise and your plan will alter again. Be flexible, record what you need and stay attentive to participants in the research settings.

* Begin where you are at.

Where data gathering begins is dependent on such things as the researcher's familiarity with the topic, the depth of the reflections, the types of questions developed, the access to information and comfort with the topic. It is a mistake for a researcher to try to be different than she / he is. It is imperative that the researcher identify the starting position in her / his conceptual baggage and monitor the changes in her/his questions and perceptions as the research progresses.

> **Kate**: My research question was formed from a problem I encountered when I suggested presenting feminist theory in a contemporary social theory course. However, it was only through living with

the data, moving back and forth exploring the voices of the women I had interviewed, that I really began to understand the origins of my questions. As the research developed I discovered links between my own questions about feminist social theory and conflicts between academic and grassroots community agendas, between academic theory and community practice.

* Be attentive and be ready to record information throughout the research process.

Data comes from a variety of sources. Fragments or snippets of conversation that may appear to have no immediate bearing on the data can become central to the analysis. Even while you may be attentive to the main sources of data (research participants) new information can come from completely unexpected sources. You must assume that **talk is serious**, and whether you are concluding an interview, tabulating survey results or laboriously combing through documents, **talk** abounds. Listening for and recording seemingly insignificant chatter can provide new directions for research and breathe new life into old material.

> **Robbie**: After each interview we continued to talk. My reflections on the interviews were as much concerned with these after-talks as with the taped interviews.

* Share the data gathering load.

Information can come from all sides and can just as easily slip away. It is simply too easy for the researcher to get immersed. The sheer volume of data, even on relatively straightforward topics, makes comprehensive analysis difficult. If you can share the data gathering efforts with collaborators, the load is lightened. Also you can discuss the research process with other researchers and with research participants. Often, the outsider view is just enough to get you out of a muddle and back into clear thinking again.

> **Robbie**: Throughout the research I met with my sister, students / researchers and our guide. For me these were "researchers anonymous" sessions. Every week I was inspired by what was shared. Inspirations would ebb through the week as I plunged myself further into the participation with International Women's Day events which only seemed to add chaos and confusion to my research. These weekly "researchers anonymous" meetings were essential for me.

However, in certain research situations, collaboration may hinder the data gathering and analysis. You may find this occurs if your research question is related to a painful experience in your life. In these situations you may find it easier to explore the topic after you make a decision not to share your research data or analysis with others until after the research is completed.

Catherine: Sandi suggested sitting down to write about the incest experience with the intention of showing it to no one. It was surprising what a difference that made. It was not so much in *what* I wrote as in *how* I wrote and the framework it gave me. I now had a choice – my very own choice about what I wrote or didn't write about.

* *Follow your instincts.*

There is little room for indecision in research. If you think there is some useful information not yet tapped, you will need to gather it. If something needs doing, do it. Often information does not present itself in manageable ways at convenient times; as a researcher you will have to adjust to gathering data when it is available. Occasionally, researchers will say "I can't detach myself. I shouldn't be feeling this way." Record these instances in your reflections, thereby accounting for yourself in the research process. This reaffirms you, the feelings you have and the negotiation that continually occurs between researcher and method.

* *Ask quality questions.*

Good questions are the hallmark of good research. If you are involved in face-to-face interviewing, the way in which you ask questions is as important as their order, their focus or the manner in which you set up an interview. Your interview guide should be a series of questions organized around the research question. During an interview, you can be flexible enough to rearrange them or perhaps leave one or two out.

For surveys, interviews and some participant observations, researchers ask the research participants questions in a direct fashion. The questions need to be thoughtfully ordered. A good question to start with is one that ascertains that the research participant has the experience you, the researcher, are interested in finding out more about. Questions that are deemed easier to answer are better placed early in interview guides. Questions that are of a sensitive nature can be placed later. As always, participants have the option of not responding or of not having their response recorded.

Occasionally, a research participant will ask to see the interview guide before an interview or the research plan before a participant observation. In the more traditional research methods, such requests must usually be denied. In this method, however, the researcher can choose to consider the request and negotiate with the participant. Subsequent to this, the focus of the questions might change, and as a result there might be a better interview.

* *Learn to listen.*

Quality research has as much to do with good listening as with good questions. When you are asking questions, the silence that sometimes follows is a thinking time for the research participants. **Listening means not being afraid**

of SILENCES. And, since asking questions and listening is meaningful discourse, it is easy to see why listening is an essential and critical component of
researching. Further, in the direct approach to data gathering, many different
individuals will have information for you. Listen to what is said and to what is
not said. Developing these listening skills will ensure that you are able to hear
and understand what is being shared with you.

Note: A research participant may provide an account of a situation that
in the eyes of the researcher is "untrue." There are distortions and inaccura-
cies in all information, and the researcher will need to decide whether to
check the information against fact or to accept the participant's account as
one the participant accepts and knows to be true. In the method of researching from the margins, it is the perceptions of the participants that are being
sought, their understanding of their social reality. Be prepared to listen to and
hear the participants' story of *their* reality.

* Be honourable and ensure that asking back can occur.
Research is about doing the best investigating you can. Since research is a
dynamic enterprise, it is difficult to make absolute promises about, for
example, the management of material or the way in which someone's voice
will appear in the analysis. Attempt to make the best decisions you can with
the information that you have, ensuring that you **could justify such decisions to the participants if asked**.

Asking back is where participants have opportunities throughout the
data gathering to make enquiries about the research and / or the researcher.
For example, in response to the researcher's question about areas missed
during an interview, a participant may seek personal advice or raise a question asking for the personal opinion of the researcher. There is an optimal
level of asking back which frequently leads to a richer and more meaningful
description of participants' experiences. Too much asking back may mean
straying from the original purpose of data gathering.

** Gathering data from research participants whom we know well is much
more difficult.*
Although this may seem odd, it is true that many researchers have difficulty
in face-to-face research encounters with people they know. Researchers are
gathering information. The tendency between familiar individuals is to fall
back on familiar interaction patterns — patterns that are often counter-
productive to data gathering.

This can also occur if more than one research participant is interviewed
simultaneously. The participants develop a special kind of interaction
between them that is different from the kind of rapport that can occur during
a one-to-one interview. However, the methodology of researching from the

margins is based on a need to challenge the structurally-imposed isolation, invisibility and silence that surround the lives of those on the margins. Because of this, the opportunities for research participants to share and make connections with others who share similar experiences and concerns is considered a priority. Group interviews can be a way of getting the word out, especially if they are used after the initial analysis has been shared with the research participants. They can be thought of as a way of adding another layer of data.

* *Get close to the data.*
The method of researching from the margins requires researchers to invest their own experience and Self in the research enterprise. If the researcher has been well-schooled in the more traditional research methods, falling back on old methods is always a risk. Do not be afraid to incorporate yourself, your emotions and your experience into the research process.

* *Stop gathering information and take a pause when you become inundated or when there is a substantial degree of repetition in the material being gathered.*
Traditional methods often rely on numbers – numbers of participants, completed surveys, days or experiences recorded. Researching from the margins relies on saturation of information. When the information gets repetitive, the researcher can do one of two things. You can choose to withdraw from data gathering for a period of time until the data feels like it is within reach again, or you can explore a new tangent and continue to gather new information.

* *Review of the literature may occur late in the research enterprise.*
If a review of published materials on the research topic is deemed necessary, the researcher can review them at any time in the research process. There is no requirement that hypotheses come from previous research. Rather, if information is considered useful, it can be added into the general analytical framework although it has no more (or less) analytical value than any other information. It is, however, important to remember that secondary sources (i.e., the literature review) are no substitute for active research. If you have explored the research topic thoroughly, your data will speak with its own authority. In the method of researching from the margins, it is best that you have a firm grasp of what your data says before you review other information.

* *Celebrate researching.*
Research is about the creation of new knowledge. Such creation is worth celebrating. Take the time to appreciate and take note of your progress,

applauding yourself for research well done and identifying areas where you can improve. If the research is a collaborative effort, plan a time for bringing the research efforts to a close in a celebration of common effort and achievement. Share your success as you would the difficulties.

3. Collecting and recording the data.

Data can range from brief notes on dated scraps of paper to complete word-by-word and gesture-by-gesture transcripts. It can also consist of audio and video recordings, descriptions of settings and observations, and public and private documents. Some of the recorded data are informal, the results of chance conversations or realizations. Others are formal, recorded observations.

The researcher's key recording responsibility consists of accurately and thoroughly documenting the information gained. Resist the temptation to interpret material at the early stages of data gathering.

> **Andrea:** I have to free myself from the notion that I know what they are trying to tell me. I keep wanting to fill in the blanks and then I don't listen as much as I should.

Record accurately and with as little interpretation as possible. Each time you catch yourself interpreting, make a note in the margin of the record. That way you are always accounted for in the research records and no ideas are lost. This means carrying your field notes at all times, keeping dated records of the research in progress ... really living with the data.

It is important to **write down your reflections immediately after an interview or data gathering experience**. In these reflections you need to identify the context and location of the data gathering. Record how you experienced the process, noting any tensions and moments when connections or insights occurred. Write up any asides that were not formally recorded and what was said at the end of the interview after the tape was turned off. Although these comments cannot be directly quoted, they often offer keen insight about the research question. Mention any changes in your data gathering plan, questions that were reordered or omitted, good probes and any new questions that were not part of the original schedule but which were more successful.

Keep records of all steps of the research process. For example, keep track of decision-making about the research focus and early refinement of the research question. Date and place the information in a file labelled PROCESS.[1] Information about the actual organization of interviews, of data sites for

---

1. There are a number of different files described in Chapter Six that will be very helpful in organizing your data.

participant observation, life histories and unobtrusive measures and of recording methods also goes into this file so that when the research reporting begins, the record of all process decisions is located in one place. Reflections on how a data gathering session went should be written up and filed here.

So too, any sorting and ordering of research questions for a survey or interview should be dated and retained in the file labelled PROCESS. Final copies of the survey and cover letter or the interview guide can be placed in this file too. A record of any steps taken to ensure better return rates or identification of potential research participants are put here. Notes taken during interviews (jottings, key words, points to question, landmarks) and post-interview comments about content go in this file as well.

Another file can be labelled CONTENT. Begin this file by putting the field notes in it. These dated notes contain comments and musings which have by now grown to a full and complete log of observations and events. These take considerable time, effort and, most of all, discipline. They are a superior method for organizing large volumes of data and later become a rich source of data for analysis. As you gather data from research participants, copies of **raw data** can be added (e.g., interview transcript copies or completed survey copies).

4. Reflecting on the data.

Different types of recordings are useful for different types of analysis. The method of researching from the margins requires a lot of reflection on the part of the researcher. This means that in addition to the regular data records, there needs to be a place for the researchers' ongoing reflections.

Reflections on content[2] are the beginning of the evolving analysis. The researcher's thoughts become ever more focussed on the themes (threads of thought) which run through the data. The focus on the content is very specific. Reflections recorded beside the content often would not necessarily make sense if they were removed from the immediate context. Such reflections are data-specific and substantive in nature.

Reflections on process are equally important to the overall analysis of data. The following examples illustrate some researchers' reflections:

Colleen: The library showed me not only how I do research but that I live my life in the same way. I recorded next to nothing on the content side of the page. The whole process of what I had done was therefore missing. My experience of raising children is similar;

---

2. There are numerous examples provided in this book of researcher's reflections on content. Chapter Six contains the section on analysis of the content that highlights the use of such reflections.

people ask my advice and I am less than helpful because I forget the particulars. I have more of a feel for the overall experience.

Brenda W.: What does 'inarticulate' mean? Does it mean 'not articulate,' or does it mean the speaker is not going to say what we want to hear? Is this another screening device which we as researchers use, whether consciously or unconsciously, to collect the data we want to collect?

Flo: Because I like to look directly at the person with whom I am communicating without distraction, I felt I did not master the technique of jotting notes throughout the interviews.

Below are more reflections that researchers jotted in their field notes.

- I have to question what I asked; did I get what I thought I wanted?
- I must stop gathering data now and analyze, even though the data says "gather more, gather more."
- I expected conclusions, I am only going to get a bit of an answer; there are so many more questions.

Continuing throughout to reflect on the research process enables you to become more skillful and intuitive as a researcher.

SUMMARY AND CHECKPOINTS

Throughout this chapter, we have presented the data gathering and recording strategies. It is important to remember that, even with willing participants available, it still takes good questions **and self-discipline** to gather good information.

We encourage you to remain close to the research focus while you are data gathering. This can be a very exciting experience for new researchers and it is tempting to enjoy the experience of being a data gatherer so much that you forget that you are seeking specific information about the research topic. Record carefully and reflect often on both the process and the content of the research experience to help you stay on track.

We recognize that the method we choose influences the type of data gathering and analysis we do, just as data gathering and analysis inform the process. The dynamic relationship between the process and the content is essential to the discovery of new information. Be focussed and be flexible.

Checkpoints

- In what ways can I maintain my data gathering focus?
- When I begin to gather data, what is data and what is not data?

- What do I do with questions that I asked but were not part of the data gathering schedule?
- How is the data to be recorded? Is there data that I have been unable to record? Why? How can I correct that?
- Why is it important to write up interview experiences, for example, immediately after thay are completed?
- Why is it necessary to reflect on the content of what is gathered and on the process of researching?
- How do I, the researcher, account for myself in the data gathering process?

CHAPTER SIX

Preparing for and Doing Analysis

getting ready
getting focussed
gearing up for data gathering
planning for data gathering
gathering data
preparing for and doing analysis ✔
presenting the analysis

INTRODUCTION

This chapter describes how to organize and analyze the data. In researching from the margins, a large volume of data can be gathered in a short time. This chapter will help you to organize this mass of data into manageable parts or categories and to make sense of each category and of each category's relation to the whole research project.

Making sense of the data, or analysis, is crucial to the overall ability of the researcher to describe and explain what is being studied. Some researchers consider analysis the most difficult of all the research steps; we think of it as the time to live with the data, to get comfortable with what it has to say and to discover the "larger, more holistic understanding. The focus is on seeing patterns / arrangements ... behind the totality of what's being studied" (Carney, 1983:58).

The schema opposite represents the overall analytical progression for the method of researching from the margins:

The schema illustrates an analysis which is based on dynamic relationships between data, between categories and the changing links between categories. Part of the dynamic is created by the researcher's efforts to simultaneously live with the data and make sense of the data. During this time, the researcher constantly reflects on both the data and the process of analyzing it. In this way, analysis emerges from the information at hand. The other part

Overall Analytical Schema

Organizing The Data
1. Observations, Reflections And Documents
2. Copies Of Data In The Form Of Bibbits

Understanding The Data:
1. Coding Bibbits Into Category Files
2. Describing The Categories Analytically
3. Living With The Data, Hurricane Thinking
4. Describing The Relationships Between Categories
5. Doing The Overall Analysis
6. Presenting The Data

of the dynamic is created by the researcher's constant moving, back and forth, between data and concepts, and between individual ideas and research explanations in order to fully describe and explain what is being researched. This keeps the researcher constantly vigilant for new understandings at all analytical points.

The great volume of data produced by the method of researching from the margins needs careful management. The basic pattern for management and for analysis is adapted from the constant comparative method, introduced in Glaser and Strauss's (1967) *The Discovery of Grounded Theory.* However, the systematic approach proposed by Glaser and Strauss has been elaborated on to give priority to two essential components of research from the margins.

First, research from the margins requires **intersubjectivity**: an authentic dialogue between all participants in the research process in which all are respected as equally knowing subjects. When managing and analyzing the data, this means that priority will be given to the voices from the margins. Each bit of data will be given equal opportunity to speak in the analysis; data will be linked with questions raised from the data. Contributions from documentation and existing theory will be included later in the process, and feedback and confirmation of analytical concepts will be solicited from research participants and collaborators familiar with the research focus.

Second, research from the margins requires **critical reflection on the social context**. Critical reflection involves an examination of the social reality "within which people exist and out of which they are functioning" (Finson, 1985:117), for that is "the real, concrete context of facts" (Freire, 1985:51). In other words, context is the fabric or structure in which the research, or the research participants' experiences, has occurred. It only makes sense that if we are to fully understand the data and effect change, we must try to understand contextual patterns and how they are sustained and controlled.

The reasons why intersubjectivity and critical reflection are **both** essential becomes clear if we look at two examples from Anne's research. Her research focussed on the question "How and under what conditions do women decide to leave an abusive marriage?" She discovered that it never occurred to some of the women that abusive treatment was not their fault or that such abuse was not deserved. One woman, who had left her marriage after twenty-five years, still blamed herself:

> I allowed myself to become a victim in a psychologically abusive marriage.

During another interview, a woman who had been a victim of physical abuse for eight years described how she was afraid to tell anyone because all her friends had good, happy marriages and because she thought it was her fault that her husband beat her.

> After he beat me, I would become very quiet and ask myself "Where did I go wrong ... maybe if I was smarter or prettier or a better cook or younger he wouldn't have to beat me."

When Anne presented her research analysis, she was careful to contextualize the women's words by referring to how historical attitudes toward women, the role of the church, the institution of marriage, peer pressure, the ideologies of self-sacrifice and romantic love, the economy, the assumptions and intricacies of criminal and family law, as well as the delivery system of social services create and legitimize abuse of women and then blame women for that abuse.

Giving priority to intersubjectivity and critical reflection on the social context throughout the analysis ensures that we are able to hear and affirm the words and experiences of the research participants and at the same time be able to critically reflect on the structures that influence the actualities of their lives.

ORGANIZING THE DATA

1. Managing the data

The general analytical design consists of examining how data items and groupings of data items generate specific and general patterns. This is done primarily through the constant comparison of data items with other data items until sections that "go together with" or "seem to help describe something" can be identified and located together in a category file.

This analysis is an ongoing process. The analysis and data collection continually overlap (i.e., whenever the researcher records reflections on either the content or the process of the research, analysis is taking place). In this chapter, the process by which all the data and reflections are brought into an integrated analysis is presented.

In Chapter Five, it was suggested that you house the data in two files, the PROCESS FILE and the CONTENT FILE. In addition to your conceptual baggage file, these files contain raw data – the foundation of the whole process of analysis. Now, decisions must be made about the nature of the accumulated data and how it can best be housed for subsequent analysis. This process is called managing the data.

The following graphic illustrates the equal importance of these two files.

Data Files

Content File	Process File
matters relating to substance	matters relating to plans and data gathering
reflections on this	reflections on this
conceptual baggage related to content	conceptual baggage related to process

2. Expanding the files

As the data gathering activites draw to an end, an expansion of the number of files will facilitate analysis of the large amount of data the research process has generated. We suggest you open the following files: a) **identity,** b) **tape,** c) **document,** d) **content** and e) **process.**[1] Each is described below. Remember, the expansion of the file structure is to *order* the data, not to change the nature of that data.

(a) Identity file

This file contains the information that identifies your research participants. A list of research participants, their names and their coded or altered identity should be kept in this file. It might look like this:

A001	John Burns, Toronto called Alan
A002	Johanna Alcott, Regina called Susan
C001	Alice Greaves, Guelph called Lisa
C002	Gayle Johnson, Victoria called Joansie
A003	Guylaine Renault, La Salle called Danielle
C003	Doug Williams, St. John's called D.J.

1. There is also an **analytical file** which is discussed in the *understanding the data* section immediately following this *organizing the data* section.

Then, each research participant should be listed on a separate index card that gives you a snapshot of that individual, information you might need to facili- tate feedback or confirm who you contacted and how many times about what. For ethical reasons, this file is kept separate from any files where con- tent is housed. This preserves the separation of the participants from the data gathered from them. Use identifying codes only to remind yourself where each bit of data originated.

An index card with contact information and comments about the inter- view might look like this:

Interview #_____   Date:_____
                                                      Place:_____
                                              Time arrive:_____
                                                      Leave:_____

  Contact: number, time
            address, telephone
  Other contact times:

  Comments: (any immediate comments about
  interview, or follow-up commitments).

Identity file contents:

  - contact code number, address, telephone number
  - contact person, if applicable
  - information relevant to the research arrangements
  - record of each contact date with individual and reason for
    contact
  - primary coding sheet for all participants

(b) Tape file

This file contains the video and / or audio tape recordings you may have made. These are to be coded by number rather than name (e.g., tape #001), and the coding sheet is to be housed in the identity file. In an effort to pre- serve anonymity, the tape file is kept separate from the identity file.

  Tape file contents:

  - video tapes coded
  - audio tapes coded

(c) Document file

This file contains dated **original research materials**, excluding the audio and / or video tapes that are in the tape file. As you manage the data, only **copies** of material can be removed from the document file for insertion into other files. This way, after data has been copied for multiple filing, the original context can always be determined. Without maintaining this reference point the material gathered can become fragmented and remain unwieldy. This is important to remember.

When data gathering is completed, original transcripts of interviews, the survey results or the observation records are housed in this file. Conceptual baggage is also placed in the document file too. Specifically, those notes about content that researchers prepare as the first step in finding a research focus, and any reflections on them, belong in the document file. Ongoing field notes and any documents (research articles, newspaper accounts, etc.) are also placed here.

Document file contents:

- conceptual baggage
- *original* field notes – notes and quotes
- *original* transcripts or completed questionnaires
- documents – articles, books, letters, diaries, periodicals, clippings, review of literature, etc.

(d) Content file

This file contains **copies** of original data: the field notes, conceptual baggage, transcripts and the like. Any data that relates to what is asked, heard and reported is included here.

Content file contents:

- *copies* of conceptual baggage, field notes, transcripts and / or completed questionnaires
- *copies* of reflections on content
- *copies* of general references
- *copies* of coded sections after new copies have been placed in category files

(e) Process file

This file contains a record of each step taken in the research process and the reflections you, the researcher, may have on the process. The information is

dated and ordered chronologically. Information about contacts with participants and information about prospective data sites fit here. So do steps such
as the development of the interview guide, the survey, or the organization of
group interviews. All *decisions* about the way the research is done are
recorded here.

Process file contents:

- account of development of research process
- interview guide, schedule, changes to either, and reflections on
  the process
- survey development, plan for conducting the survey, changes to
  either, reflections on process
- comments on data gathering, reflections on process
- comments on researcher in the data gathering process (how you
  organized it and handled it, what might need to change)

For example:

Process	Reflections
Jan 16	
Focussed on question, got help from friend, talked it through until it became clear.	it helps to collaborate what if they don't want to share that?
The research focus is going to be something like "how do women on welfare feel about the word welfare?"	

At this point in the research process, all information that has been collected should be housed in files. Though this does not mean that data gathering is completely finished, it should be far enough along that the management files are well stocked and the process of analysis can begin. As data
gathering concludes, the information can simply be added to the appropriate
files.

3. Preparing the analysis

Analysis involves living with and making sense of the large amount of data
available through the method of researching from the margins. The schema
presented earlier in the chapter is the guide. The first part of the schema

identifies file management functions; the second part of the schema identifies the files of analysis.

These are the terms used:

Bibbits – loose bits of data, sections of data
Properties – elements of categories
Categories – elements of substantive theory
Substantive Theory – elements of grand theory
Grand Theories

The data needs to be prepared for analysis. Because of the dynamic nature of the analysis suggested, the data must be able to constantly move in relation to other data. The following schema, adapted from the constant comparative method presented by Glaser and Strauss (1967) will help you understand how and why data are compared.

Overall Schema For Constant Comparison Of Data

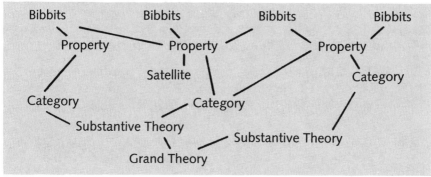

To do analysis, the data must be divided into portions that are manageable. The continuous process of comparison and linking of **bibbits** helps researchers to understand the specific and overall properties, patterns and relationships between data and between groups of data. These form the initial bases of the analysis.

> **Bibbit:** a passage from a transcript, a piece of information from field notes, a section of a document or snippet of conversation recorded on a scrap of paper that can stand on its own but, when necessary, can be relocated in its original context.

The data must be divided into bibbits in preparation for coding and cross-referencing before it can be located in category files. Each **bibbit** (piece, snippet or bite of information) needs to be photocopied so that it can be put into as many category files as its content and context require.

Each bibbit should be able to stand on its own, that is, make sense when it is separated from its context. Some bibbits may be quite large (e.g., several pages of description of one event) while others may be very small (e.g., a two sentence section cut out from a transcribed interview). However, to maintain the integrity of the entire research project, the bibbit must be identified in such a way that it can be quickly and easily relocated within its home context. This can be done in a number of ways.

Bibbits may be colour coded or numbered or marked to ensure relocation if needed. For example, look at the following bibbit. It is four sections long and marked by a code.

R11S33 Sandi: And now she is empowered in front of that system. And can say "I can't do it that way and I won't do it that way. This is a better way." So the education is far beyond the doing of a piece of research or the changes in one individual. It's sort of a radiating ...

R11B33 Becky: Well, there aren't many fields and not many places within academia which will accept that.

R11S34 Sandi: Does that mean undoing, like you said, do we throw it out?

R11B34 Becky: 'Cause I know I was doing something in scripture and it was like "Find the intent of the author. I don't care what it means to you." And it's like going through the whole hermeneutical thing, who knows what the author intended? Nobody knows. There is this preconceived idea that we can get to that, uncover that by reconstructing the social milieu of the day.

The code indicates that the bibbit was taken from interview R11 (eleventh interview in residence) and the section is Sandi's 33rd comment, Becky's 33rd comment, Sandi's 34th comment and Becky's 34th comment. The bibbit can always be quickly located within the R11 interview transcript by the 33rd and 34th notations.

Here is another example of coding:

Well, with Jim, Jim knows ... well I got him now that he knows that I get a check once a month, like he doesn't know it's Social Assistance but he knows that when he asks for his hot chocolate and his Fruit Loops, that he has to wait for check day. 1.02 / S

The author has marked this bibbit to indicate that it came from data source 1, page 2, and S is who has been transcribed.

Here is a third, quite ingenious, method of coding:

FNFeb17 I overheard the following comments made by junior high students who had stopped for a cigarette at the bus stop. I was waiting in the bus shelter with my daughter. They were waiting for someone to join them. She was coming down the street toward them and they commented that she'd worn the same clothes a couple of days ago.

* * * * *

(red star,@#$@#$)

Girl #1 She wore that outfit on Monday.
Girl #2 Yeah, her Mom's on welfare.
Girl #3 No, she isn't, is she?
Girl #2 Sure she is. Go ask her.
Girl #3 (Screeching down the street) Susan, is your MOM on welfare?
Girl #4 Course not, she's got a job!
Girl #2 She is so on welfare. You got nothing but toilet paper and Kraft Dinner in your house.
Girls all started to chant toilet paper Kraft Dinner, toilet paper Kraft Dinner ...

The bibbit is pulled from the field notes (FN) recorded on Feb 17 and cut to be located in a category file once it is coded. The #$@#$ indicates that it was an angry exchange and that swear words had been left out of the field notes. The red star means there were lengthy reflections by the recorder on the particular scenario. Whatever the codes, the researcher must always be able to recontextualize the bibbit quickly and efficiently.

Glaser and Strauss (1967) say that bits of data, what we call bibbits, are one of the stepping stones to the development of grounded theory. Other stepping stones are properties, categories and substantive theory.

Properties are characteristics of bibbits, the themes or identifiers which are located within a bibbit. Each bibbit may have several properties.

Categories are groups of bibbits which have common properties and seem to "go together." These cannot be described until the category contains enough information.

Substantive theories are theories developed from the categorized data that help to describe and explain the research focus. These theories remain close to the data.

These stepping stones lead you to:

Grand theory, the more formal and much more distant-from-the-data theory. (Substantive theory remains close to the data.[2])

For the purposes of this analysis, we are primarily concerned with properties, categories and the links between categories. Any conceptual development, that is the linking of categories, can be called the beginnings of substantive theory.

One more key word used in analysis of data is **saturation.**

Saturation occurs when added information does not reveal new understanding about relations or abstractions.

A category is said to be saturated when the addition of new bibbits does not alter the overall complexion of the category. In other words, additional information does not add to the richness and density of the category description.

When categories are saturated, there is enough information to make statements with a comfortable degree of certainty. Just as categories get saturated, so do substantive theories. When no new links between categories emerge, the analytical development at that point in the data gathering is exhausted. When the analytical files have reached saturation, statements about links between categories can be made with confidence. If no saturation occurs, statements about the tendencies within categories or links between categories can be made.

UNDERSTANDING THE DATA

1. Analyzing the data

One more set of files is needed. These are the **analysis files,** established for the purpose of bringing information into relation with other information until patterns begin to emerge. In these files, mulitiple bits of information, ideas and notes are grouped together according to the constant comparative method. The bibbits you have identified are coded and then placed with similar bibbits of data.

(a) The analysis files: content

These files consist of a collection of file folders labelled with different codes (representing category names). Similar bibbits of information, information with identical coding, are housed within a single file folder.

---

2. Glaser and Strauss (1967:3) indicate that theory must still be able to assist in a) the production and explanation of behaviour, b) the theoretical advance of sociology, c) the provision of a perspective on behaviour (a stance on the data), d) the provision of and a guide for a style of research on particular areas of behaviour, and e) the understanding of practical situations.

Coding refers to the identification of an idea, event, theme or common property that identifies the content of a bibbit. As the researcher codes data, she / he is methodically labelling events and behaviours for further analysis. She / he is an essential element of the coding activity; this alone reaffirms the interpretive nature of research (see Introduction).

Code labels are developed by the researcher to represent the code category. Code names may alter as the material in the category expands. So, too, the areas between the codes may become shady and blurred as two categories show their affinity for one another or their common content. The longer a researcher lives with the codes, the more settled and clear they become. No one other than the researcher need be familiar with the codes.

Placement of similarly coded bibbits into the same location is called filing. The location becomes identified as a CATEGORY. If a bibbit is identifiable by more than one code, copies of the same bibbit are placed in each appropriate file category.

Categories coded on bibbit:
A = arrest record
B = break and enter
C = incarceration

Copies of bibbit are placed in 3 different files marked by codes
A   B   C

For example:

#007 / 80-84

R1 I am very disappointed and have no trust at all and I am not a believer in our Olympic association because they went along with the Moscow boycott. They didn't have the guts to say
W1 "We're going!" God I ached to go. I've blown it, you know. 1980 would have been my last chance at a medal.

codes:

R1 (retirement circumstances)
W (will or desire to compete)
#007 (interview number seven, transcript part 80-84)

Two copies were made, one for file *R1* and one for file *W*. The original bibbit is put back in the content file, next to the copy of the interview transcript #007.

The codes emerge from the data. That is, when you look closely at a section of a transcript like the one above and have the research question in your mind, what is important will emerge. In the example of interview #007, the research question was about how female Olympians leave high performance sport. The bibbit, or section of the transcript, brings two points to mind: first, the boycott had something to do with the retirement and second, she really wanted to compete but couldn't.

The bibbit may well undergo further analysis later. Suppose the researcher realizes after coding a number of interviews that the Moscow boycott seems to be popping up with great regularity. This indicates that a new category called **B80** (BOYCOTT 1980) might be added to the analytical files and several of the **R1** (retirement circumstances) bibbits could be copied into the **B80** file.

Here is another example of some recoding. The original bibbit was first analyzed as having four category codes:

> *C1* Why I got married? ... Um, because he got in trouble with the
>   law, and because he was looking at four years in jail again and I
> *C2* felt sorry for him.

> *Should* Yeah, I thought it would all be better afterwards, but it wasn't.
>   It got worse. I should have let him go. I paid for his lawyer and I
>   worked while he sat at home. Then after that he was using me
>   ... saying little things like "Oh, the people at work don't like
>   you, they hate you, they think you are a tramp ..." You know.
>   *F* He was messing around with my head.

> *C2* Finally I got mad enough, scared enough and beaten enough. I
>   walked out. (001:118-121)

This bibbit is coded into four different codes: *C1* (Control-power) and *C2* (Control-decision making), *Should* (Should not Want or Will) and *F* (Fear). The researcher made four copies of this bibbit, putting one in each of the four category files **(housed in her analysis file)** she had created and the extra one was returned to the **content file.** After the researcher gathered more information from other participants, she discovered that psychological battering was a theme in some of the data. She returned to this bibbit in the content file, recoded it to include **psych** and then relocated all the other bibbits, in their respective category locations, and added the new code for cross-referencing.

There are various ways of doing the coding. Coding conventions are not yet well established and, at this point, seem to consist of "it seems to fit" or "it belongs" or "the bibbits go together." Occasionally, a perfect bibbit is found which becomes a definitive part of a category. The best coding comes from knowing the data and being able to move it about comfortably and wisely.

Some of the people who helped develop this method described their coding experience in the following ways. The comments shown here are bibbits from their respective process files.

> **Brenda W.**: Initially I found it difficult to code each bibbit with categories but before long, the process was running away with me and it seemed that the bits were naming themselves. The experience of naming the bibbits and placing them in the files — it sounds so simple — but it was so remarkable! As the files grow, their names are not just names anymore, they take on more and more meaning until links start to form, like little tributaries from file to file. AMAZING PROCESS.

> **Tarel**: I transcribed each interview and then made photocopies. On the side of each page I left a margin. I used this space to code my data: reading through the interviews I wrote down descriptive words to indicate the themes of the experiences that had been shared with me. I then used the same method to code my own conceptual baggage.

Brenda and Tarel both found a particular process, close to the "overall analytical schema" presented at the beginning of this chapter, to be helpful. Lorene discovered a somewhat unique approach to the analysis, one we call the stories option.

> **Lorene**: The data spoke strongly to me, so strongly, in fact, that only in their complete context could the words and categories speak to me. I found that if I removed bibbits of information from the context it broke the flow and the rhythm I felt from the words.
>
> Because the women's experiences were a guide for me, I let myself look at each interview as a story. Sometimes stories have headings, so I combed through each story and picked out what I thought the headings would be. Certain words and phrases repeated themselves in each of the stories. I did a second layering of these words and phrases, using a coloured highlighter, and then combed through a third time using a different colour again. The phrases or words that captured the most attention became my categories.

Lorene had to search for a different way to hold her data together. Rather than physically dissect the stories into bibbits, she highlighted the descriptors

still held firmly in the text. These became "categories" even though no separate categorical files were organized. The "categories" then were woven
together into analytical themes. Thus, she eventually brought the themes
together without cutting copies of the stories. The integrity of her stories was
maintained yet she was still able to draw the common themes out and
describe her data. This stories option, as Lorene developed it, is possible only
if the physical size of the information gathered is small enough, and the
researcher familiar enough with it to keep the entire picture of information in
focus throughout the analysis. As in the other examples, Lorene's data took
precedence over the process.

How many categories are appropriate? Well, the number is totally
dependent upon the data and the researcher's insight into what the data
indicates. For example:

> **Kate**: I developed quite a large number of categories from my
> research material but subsequently realized that each category was
> so specific that there was very little information eligible to be placed
> in them. When I began to think of categories in a more general way I
> was able to focus in on 14 categories.

The topic of her work was the study of feminism as a paradigm rather than a
critique of existing paradigms within sociology. Kate's categories were:

C1 Change	M1 Methodology
C2 Conflict	PP Personal / Political
DS Descriptions of Sociological Theory	P1 Praxis / Goals
E1 Epistemology	RD Roots / Debts
F1 Factors	SP Starting Point
FA Feminist Assumptions	S1 Strategies
FC Feminist Critique	U1 Unique

Sandi: Originally, some coded categories were defined too early in the research process. That is, the categories were defined too much by imported data and theory. This resulted not only in a considerable waste of time and effort, but also created categories in which the data did not fit. Once I recognized the problem, I called the categories a false start, laid them aside and began sorting and resorting all over again. I ended up with 54 categories, some very full and others quite thin.

Sandi's topic was "how and under what conditions female athletes leave high performance sport." Here is a sampling of the categories emergent from her research:

A1 Age	I1 Idols
B1 Body Image	I3 Injuries
B2 Boycott	I4 Interview comments
B3 Boyfriend / girlfriend / sibling	M1 Marriage
C1A Work / sport / retire	M2 Mentor
C1B Finances / sport / retire	M3 Motherhood
C1G Life in general / sport / retire	M4 Medals / results
C3 Comeback	M5 Media
D1 Disjunctures / Out of Step	R2 Retirement / sport
E1 Ethics	R3 Recall problems
F4 Future goals	S1 Schooling
F6 Female testing	S2 Sexuality
F7 Feminism	S61 Personal sport history

Categories emerge from the data, and although the number of categories could be quite high, it is important to remember that categories are used in order to bring bits of data into a physical relationship. Too many categories can be counter-productive to analysis. If there is not enough data in a category, the category may not come close to saturation, making analysis of the content difficult. Categories overloaded with *dissimilar* data are equally counter-productive. Too few categories can lead to thick files where only peripherally related bibbits are located side by side.

(b) The Analysis files: process

The process files contain information about the dynamics of the research process. Bibbits of information and reflections about doing the research are coded and placed in appropriate files. Common themes for the process files might include **rapport, analysis, problems in data gathering, time, check off lists, conceptual baggage (process), and / or interview strategies**.

Some of the process data lends itself to chronological ordering. Other bibbits are more thematic reflections on the research process. Here are some sample bibbits from the analysis files (process) of researchers:

Process
> *FN* **Colleen**: Putting down reflections is really very interesting. I find myself surprised at the distance I was able to put between myself and the data. Sometimes in making these categories I think I am jumping a step and analyzing. Some of the cross-referencing seems to jump into analysis.

Process
> *FN* **Catherine**: I thought I could not risk cutting up my data (on incest) and sticking it in different file folders. It didn't feel safe enough. However, I discovered envelopes much safer. That broke the ice and I found it was surprising how little the safety factor affected me.

FN = field notes

Colleen makes two interesting points, one about distancing herself from the data and the other about the cross-referencing leading her to analysis. Both are true and both are essential to later analysis. Catherine, on the other hand, was looking for safety rather than distance. She was uncomfortable with the physical layout of file folders. A subtle change in data management led to greater ease with the process. Both indicate that the more data was handled, the better the researchers felt about the process.

Here are other comments contained in the analysis file (process) of some people who have used the method of researching from the margins.

About handling the data:
– The more voices I hear the better I understand the meaning.

– I wanted to gather every little bibbit of data. I had to make myself stop. I was living inside the data and couldn't get enough distance from it to actually hear what it had to say to me.

– I interviewed myself to get the conceptual baggage recorded. I made a file on myself and loved it. I was scared a bit though because I didn't know how to do the write up. But I really learned a lot from the participants and a lot about myself.

About the researcher distancing her/himself from the data:
– I needed to distance myself from the data. This distance resulted in an inability to write down my reflections concerning the data I had collected. My reflections were limited by what I was able to allow in at one time because I knew my life would be changing from this experience.

About coding and recoding:
– I wish I had accounted for the process better. There is so much I thought but so little I recorded. Now, I can't piece it all together. I can't remember when or why I did that.

– How do I separate my reflections from the data? I don't want to be interpreting what they are saying to me. I want to give their voices the priority.

About making sense of the data:
– I find that the research question I was asking was not what I really got at. They were telling me about *what* kinds of choices they made and I was asking about *how* they made them.

As is evidenced above, the coding of process is vital to all further analytical work. All material in the process file is eligible for coding. In all likelihood, the data will have to be read and re-read until the beginnings of a coding system emerge. Coding is emergent. Time is needed for the categories to emerge.

(c) Analysis within data categories:

The analysis of data contained in categories is the first step to consolidating information. Each of the analysis content and process files can now be described on the basis of what is inside. The initial category descriptions could consist of a point-by-point outline of what is contained in the file. Or, a paragraph outlining the file contents can be written and attached to the file. These initial descriptions will serve as temporary summaries of file contents until such time as the data gathering and the coding of bibbits is concluded.

Not all bibbits will fit comfortably within categories. If the bibbits help explain the category, they belong there. If they are not helpful to the category's description, it may be that they do not fit the developing sense of the category or are indicative of areas where the category has not yet reached saturation. If some bibbits simply cannot be placed they are called satellites. Such bibbits sometimes indicate directions for further research, pointing to categories that need particular attention. Other times, such bibbits are simply unique bits of information that need to be reported as such.

The number of bibbits in a category is not a sure measure of the strength of a category. It is saturation that is the measure of strength. This is reached when other bibbits are added to the category in question but do not add any new dimensions to the description.

(d) Analysis between data categories

In essence, analysis consists of moving data from category to category (constant comparative), looking for what is common (properties) and what is uncommon (satellites) within categories and between categories. The data is arranged and rearranged until some measure of coherence becomes evident. The patterns which emerge from the comparisons can then be shared with some of the participants.

At this stage of the research process, the researcher brings all categories (saturated and unsaturated) together and tries to identify where the links exist between them. There is no attempt in the analysis to reach a particular level of abstraction. It is the data that determines what analysis is possible and what experiences and concepts can ultimately be described.

Cross-referencing:
Since all the bibbits placed in categories are cross-referenced, a good place to start looking for categories which "go together" is the cross-referencing. In the example of the retiring female athletes, the two codes **R1** and **W** are cross-referenced on each copy of the bibbit. These are clues to possible patterns. If many of the bibbits in a category have a similar pattern of cross-referencing, it may well be a strong pattern. Similarly, if bibbits in a category definitely do not cross-reference with particular other categories, there is a pattern there also. As the category files are moved about to be brought into proximity each with the other, look for trends, for matchings or for obvious mismatchings. These patterns are the beginnings of categorical linkings or concept building.

Hurricane thinking:
One strategy for understanding links between categories uses an approach called hurricane thinking. The research question is written in the centre of a page. This is the "eye of the hurricane." Category names on little cards are

moved about the page until those which have the strongest ties remain closest to the centre and those with less obvious or weaker ties sit at a distance. Then lines (linkages) are drawn between each category and the centre, with darker lines denoting stronger links. After repeating this process several times, a researcher who knows the data well will be able to see patterns of relations which, at least temporarily, will describe the data.

Tarel: The categories "marriage" and "career" were the focal points of these young women. I decided to place them [the categories] in the centre of the paper, creating a more logical picture for myself. The linkages between different categories were suggested by the data explicitly as well as by my own intuitive feelings.

Brenda completed two hurricane analyses, one of which she completed with one of her participants. It looked like this:

Hurricane Thinking

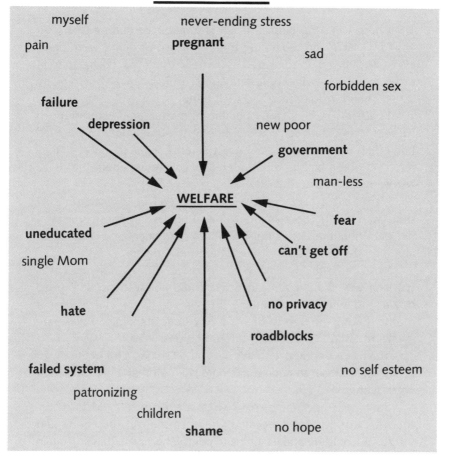

Her constant cross-comparisons and matchings led to a complex pattern which, at the initial level of analysis, is rich data loosely woven into an analytic fabric. A quick overview of the category names shows that most codes have negative connotations; there seems to be very little celebration in the scheme. Further research resulted in the strengthening of some of the categories (they are shown in bold). The pattern simplified and strengthened. For Brenda, analysis was ongoing and involved several attempts to make cross-referencing comparisons before she was able to do the hurricane thinking.

Here is another researcher's account of her analytical journey:

Robbie: I began my analyzing by going through my reflections and noting all the emotive words and phrases. I compiled quite a long list which I read through several times and then read aloud. It read something like a poem and seemed a tidy summation of the experience of the International Women's Day committee over the last four months.

I began making bibbits. It felt strange to be cutting into their words. Cutting and separating from other words didn't seem right. However, I began to think of it as a puzzle that I was taking apart in order to put it together differently, not just in one way but in many ways. Then it made sense and I felt better.

I gathered quite a crop of bibbits and attempted without much success to maintain some order among the unruly lot. This proved fairly futile as they would not be restrained. I began to feel even better about these bibbits, although mildly concerned about the chaos before me.

I still had a sense of being too general in my categories. I thought I might be missing some subtleties in these voices. I decided, nonetheless, to put them into file folders and leave them alone for awhile. I went for a walk around the park.

Working with my data was a massive struggle for me. I was working with a fluid substance which did not want to be pinned down and which I was intent on pinning down at least for a moment, long enough to derive a few understandings. I was very aware of choosing particular interpretations.

The more I worked with this data, and I shared a lot of time with it, the more I realized how much more was in it than I had chosen to work with.

So, I made up some games to help me organize the data. Then, then it came to me. It became visible to me. All the charts and puzzles and cutting and pasting and poetry, hurricane thinking again and again and the liberated pieces finally spoke! JUBILATION!

Robbie's experience was intense. Her poetic word play was ingenious and productive. She looked for words common between files and used these to describe the links between the two categories. Three are shown below:

Category file names: feminist action and post-feminism

Common words: changing perceptions challenging in-touch reality showing knowing connecting constructing anger communicating

Category file names: feminist action and feminist awareness

Common words: collective non-hierarchical support organizing changing acting constructive responsible speaking-out hearing affirmation commitment voicing anger

Category file names: doubts and feminist action

Common words: what-to-do feeling-checkmated angry nervous scared becoming-political

By finding words common to pairs of categories, Robbie was able to describe the relationship between categories.

Some data will want to speak louder than others. It is only with constant effort that the researcher is able to maintain some balance between all the bibbits in each category needing to be heard. The loudness of some data ("I had a spectacular fall and broke my leg in five places," "then he raped me") will overshadow equally important but quieter data ("she had a baby at 15," "I left the job in May because of some trouble with the boss"). However, every bibbit of data is in a dynamic relationship with others. Don't let bibbits of data take charge like some people in a group. If there is a faction that seems to speak loudly perhaps it belongs in a separate category that is closely related.

There are some bibbits of data and some categories, too, that will not appear to form links with other bibbits or categories. If things don't seem to relate, you may move the bibbit or category into a file of its own. The placement of this is dynamic, not static; after you have lived with the analysis a while longer, the relationships may become clearer. If the information resists inclusion, then it is what is referred to as a **satellite**, information that has, as yet, no place in the analysis. **Satellites** are very important indications of areas where more research is needed.

A cautionary note: in the method of researching from the margins, we look to analysis grounded in the data and to pluralist possibilities to gain meaning. The data is probed for patterns, worked, moved and worked again, until patterns present themselves. All information is useful in contributing to the general design, an overall existing pattern about the research focus.

Finally, a description of the research results can be written. It will be a first and very temporary draft description, at best an artificial closing. The summaries of each of the categories and the description of each of the links between categories (or the lack of links between categories) is the essential basis of the later interpretations.

2. Living with the data and revising the analysis

For the researcher, there is one last step in doing the analysis – that of living with the analysis for a period of time. Simply put, this means the researcher has to draw back from the analysis (Lofland and Lofland, 1984), to get some distance from it in order to reflect upon it. After a period of time has passed (one-two weeks), the researcher returns to the analysis with a fresh outlook.

Living with the data involves the following process:

- step back
- reflect on the analysis
- live with it and its implications for a while
- rework the analysis as necessary

This is clearly a time for reflection on the data, the analysis and the destination of the research. Collaborators may be called upon at this time (as Brenda did with her hurricane thinking about welfare) or the reflection can be done alone. As Carney (1983:70) writes, this is "the time to be objective about your subjectivity."

It is also the time to review the early field notes and conceptual baggage for hunches, queries and concerns. This "retreading" can respark some of the original excitement in the research project and can highlight possible connections and solutions to complex relationships that have not been clarified. Blind spots in a researcher's approach can also be identified.

The tranquility of the reflective period is a dramatic change of pace from the energetic data gathering and analytic stages of research. Researchers can take advantage of the time and space to begin to think about how the data is to be presented to participants and to a wider audience.

Here are two researchers' comments on living with the data:

> **Brenda W.**: It's just not the same me who waded in so long ago and neither is this the same spot that I waded into. Everything has changed. It looks the same on the surface but underneath it has grown in meaning and been transformed.

Brenda's realization came after a time away from the data. The perspective is critical to the way in which the analysis is developed. This conscious distancing enables the researcher to see the overall pattern, to see the forest *and* the trees, and to make adjustments on the final analysis.

Chart I

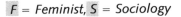
F = *Feminist, S* = *Sociology*

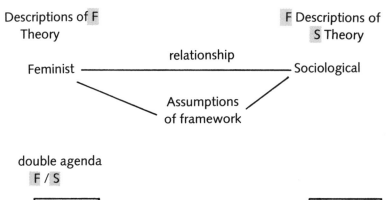

Descriptions of F
Theory

F Descriptions of
S Theory

Feminist ———————————————— Sociological

relationship

Assumptions
of framework

double agenda
F / S

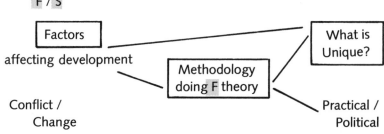

Factors

affecting development

What is
Unique?

Methodology
doing F theory

Conflict /
Change

Practical /
Political

||||||||||||||||||||||||||||||||||||||||||||||||||||||||||||||||||||||||||||||||||||||||||||||||||||

Chart II

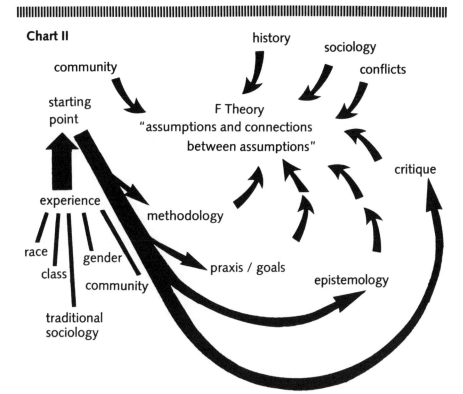

history

sociology

community

conflicts

starting
point

F Theory
"assumptions and connections
between assumptions"

critique

experience

methodology

race

gender

class

praxis / goals

community

epistemology

traditional
sociology

The second example is taken from a piece of research which began as a three-month project but grew into a project that lasted eleven months. The analysis involved considerable data, much of it theoretical. Three hurricane thinking examples are included here to illustrate how living with the data can result in changes in the analysis.

In Chart I (page 151), there are two mini-hurricanes. One shows the dialectical relationship between a description of feminist theory and a feminist description of sociological theory. The second shows the initial relationship between the categories. The category Conflict/Change is, at this point, a satellite, unlinked with other categories.

Chart II (page 151) is another version of the analysis. There is an increase in the number of categories and descriptions; the dynamic nature of the relationships is more evident. The chart is a virtual swirl of activity as categories inform each other and the general schema.

Chart III (page 153) is a version of the analysis produced after a considerable period of time living with the data. The analysis had reached a certain stability and the researcher was able to chart the relationships in a layered and complex spiral. Note the increased detail and the inclusion of descriptors on some of the linkage lines.

The analysis shown in the three charts demonstrates that, even with such complexity and evidence of emergent analysis, new information, new insights or a new observer would result in a slightly different chart again.

Since the data and the process remain dynamic, it is difficult to get exactly the same hurricane thinking result each time until very near the end of the analysis when the links are more firm and solid – the data slows down. Here are some of Kate's thought on doing this analysis:

> **Kate**: Not only did I find the bibbits of the data moved among different files, the longer I lived with various files the more they changed and developed. I found myself frustrated at times by my own desire to separate the data into clear categories "once and for all," even though I knew this totally conflicted with my experience in the everyday world. For weeks I would live with one flip chart on my wall, thinking that it was the sketch of my final analysis. Then something else would shift the focus as I read through another file or gained some insight from a new link. At that point a new web began to grow on another chart and they would keep each other company for a while. Sometimes whole files would then need to be taken apart and moved.
>
> In the end, I came to accept that, although any closure could only be artificial, I had lived with the data and one particular chart long enough to feel that I could try and let the data speak in a way that would be honourable.

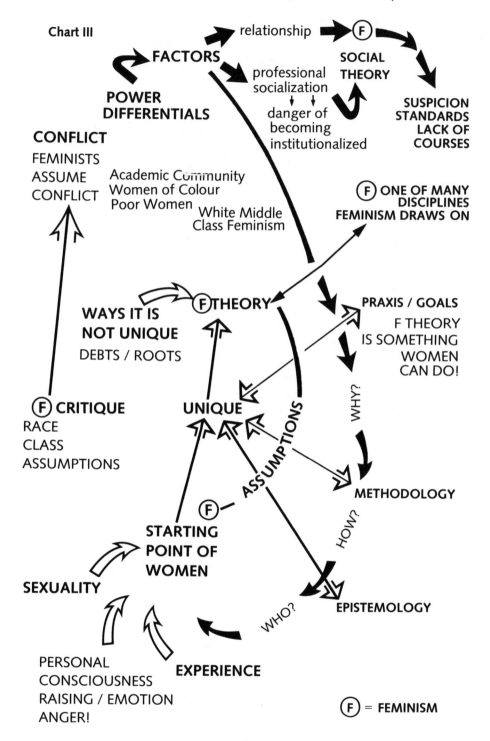

Chart III

relationship → (F) SOCIAL THEORY → SUSPICION STANDARDS LACK OF COURSES

FACTORS

POWER DIFFERENTIALS

professional socialization → danger of becoming institutionalized

CONFLICT
FEMINISTS ASSUME CONFLICT

Academic Community
Women of Colour
Poor Women   White Middle Class Feminism

(F) ONE OF MANY DISCIPLINES FEMINISM DRAWS ON

WAYS IT IS NOT UNIQUE
DEBTS / ROOTS

(F) THEORY

PRAXIS / GOALS
F THEORY IS SOMETHING WOMEN CAN DO!

(F) CRITIQUE
RACE
CLASS
ASSUMPTIONS

UNIQUE

ASSUMPTIONS

WHY?

METHODOLOGY

(F) —

STARTING POINT OF WOMEN

HOW?

SEXUALITY

WHO?

EPISTEMOLOGY

PERSONAL CONSCIOUSNESS RAISING / EMOTION ANGER!

EXPERIENCE

(F) = FEMINISM

SUMMARY AND CHECKPOINTS

This process of data analysis will help those who have accumulated a lot of data and need a way to organize it **(data management)** to make sense of it in a way that it treats the data fairly **(data analysis)**. The development of analysis through the process of living with the data and distancing yourself from it is like the weaving of a unique and rich thought cloth. The major threads are the themes running through the data. The colours are the rich descriptions gathered through observations, recordings, surveys, or other data gathering methods. Weavers concerned about the quality and integrity of their work will produce fine materials.

Checkpoints

- What are organizing files and how are they useful?
- Have I got the unmarked originals of all data filed?
- What is coding? Where does coded material go?
- When is the coding finished?
- How do I organize similarly coded information?
- After describing categories of coded information, what level of analysis have I reached?
- What is analysis of categories and of links between categories, and why is that important?
- What is cross-referencing of bibbits? What is hurricane thinking?
- After completing the analysis, why must I "live with the analysis" for awhile?

CHAPTER SEVEN

Presenting the Analysis

---

getting ready getting focussed
gearing up for data gathering
planning for data gathering
gathering data
preparing for and doing analysis
presenting the analysis ✔

INTRODUCTION

After the tasks of finding a research focus, learning data gathering skills, planning and conducting data gathering and analyzing the information have been completed, the researcher is finally ready to organize the presentation of the analysis. This chapter is divided into sections on the writing of a draft report, sharing the analysis with research participants, getting the word out and acting on what we know — moving from research to action.

PRESENTING AN ANALYSIS

Research activities are usually concluded with some sort of reporting. Although the presentation of the information may take one of a number of forms depending on what is to be reported to whom, a written document usually accompanies such presentations. Written reports serve as a public record of the research, documenting lives and experiences that too often go unrecorded. Writing some kind of report can be an important way to get the word out; a written document can become a resource for other people on the margins who share similar experiences or questions.

The writing or presenting of a research report occurs in a dynamic context. That is, the writing or presentation is an ongoing part of the analysis. The interplay between the information and the researcher continues. As you write, you must constantly go back and forth from data to analysis. As you make interpretations, "the remaining data is examined to see if and how it corroborates or refutes the ongoing analysis" (Reinharz, 1983:183).

The researcher's words are the glue that holds the report together. However, the research report must be grounded in the experience, and therefore the voices, of the participants. Their words need to be woven together with yours into a well-integrated account. The researcher's words must be as free as possible of judgement and rhetoric. The research is concerned with evaluating the data, not the participants. When the data is being described or explained, the voices of the participants need to be given priority. In this way, the researcher can provide a forum in which the experiences and thoughts of the participants can be expressed.

There are essential elements to any report. First, it is important to document the process of discovery. This includes descriptions of a) the inception of the research, b) the researcher's conceptual baggage, c) the formation of the research focus, d) the plan for data gathering, e) the overall account of the data gathering process, f) the management of the data, g) the analytical process and h) the final results. Consistent with our understanding that the creation of knowledge and praxis is political, we add to the list a further item, i) the plan for action.

Second, there needs to be a presentation of information: what was learned and how that is useful. In essence, this is where the analysis which developed from working with your analysis files is presented. Parts of each category are described and their relation to each other is explained. Written presentations of research from the margins are likely to include examples, stories, or quotes drawn from the original data. To be useful the report must be readable.

Third, new questions emerge from the analysis, some of which show directions for further research and action while others require that you return to the original research focus for a new layering of reflections and analysis.

Fourth, there is the overall evaluation of the research process and the research content, a sort of afterword which raises new questions and suggests new ways of approaching research, acting for social change and getting the word out.

Reporting on research requires some planning. An overall balance between process and content and between description and analysis is essential. Make a plan and stick to it.

1. Writing a draft

The research draft **describes the process** of data gathering and analysis, how it was done, and **presents an analysis** which is grounded in the data. The researcher must explain the data gathering process, her / his participation in the entire research process and the evaluation of data. What is gathered is eligible for description and needs explanation. All the data has a place, from documents and conceptual baggage to observations from surveys, interviews and unobtrusive recordings. We also recommend that the research draft contain a section on the researcher's reflection on the entire research enterprise.

There is more than one way to plan a research report. One way is to prepare a general outline of what is included and where different parts of the report are to be located. An overall research draft will likely parallel the manner in which the research process unfolds. For example:

Research Report
I. Describing the process
(a) Inception of the study
— Where did the research idea come from?
— How do I describe what my research is?
— Why and how did this research begin?
— What is my research focus?
— What decisions have I made about the possible directions of this research during the initial planning?

(b) Conceptual baggage
— What do I think I already know about the research focus?
— In what ways is the research important to me and why?
— What do I hope to accomplish with this research?
— What expectations or fears do I have about doing this research?
— Can I identify any external frameworks or responsibilities that may influence or shape the research?

(c) Basic research plan
— What method did I choose to use for gathering data?
— How can I best describe this method?
— How have I organized the data gathering (who, where, when)?
— What has been my specific data gathering plan, the step-by-step plan from initial to final contact with participants?

(d) Conducting the data gathering
— Was the data gathering plan appropriate? Did it work?
— How has the data been managed (transcriptions, recordings, files)?
— What reflections are recorded about the data gathering process?

(e) Preparing for and doing analysis
— What was the plan for data analysis?
— How was the data analyzed?

- Had the hurricane thinking patterns reached stability?
- Is there any left over data? If so, how can I account for it?
- How have various people participated in the analysis?

II. **Presentation of the data and analysis**

(a) Presenting the data and analysis
- Is the analytical outline grounded in the data?
- Are the properties of each category adequately described?
- Have I fully accounted for myself in the process?
- Are all the steps described; could someone else undertake similar research with this information?
- *Is the data presented comprehensively and sensitively?*
- Is the data presented so that participants can see themselves reflected in it?
- Is the reporting accurate, reliable, valid?
- Are the participants satisfied with the report?
- Am I satisfied with the report?
- Do I know what to do next?

(b) Overview of the research (initial intentions, content, process) and implications for action
- What have the participants indicated about ways to bring about social change?
- What have other interested parties indicated about action?
- Have I described, as honourably as possible, what actions are likely to bring about positive social change?
- Have I indicated what my investment in any action that comes out of the research will be?

III. **Appendix**

(a) List of files
(b) Hurricane thinking (i.e., analytical patterns)
(c) Reflections on doing research

Another way to plan a research report is to formulate questions to help focus the material. A question about the main themes of the research leads to descriptions and explanations of various themes that have emerged. For example, a question about the willingness of participants to share their experiences with the researcher would lead to an elaboration of a particular part of the research process. In any case, good organization before writing the report will facilitate organized reporting.

2. Tips on writing

a) Getting ready for analysis

There are several guidelines that can be very useful when you begin to write a draft. One good practice is to **describe**. then **explain**, content and process. By answering "What are the components of this research?" the elements of the categories can be described, as can the intra- and inter-categorical relationships.

Another good practice is to have a firm grasp of the data and the analysis before turning to secondary sources (e.g. material in the document file). The emergent sense of the research is difficult to maintain in front of the overwhelming weight of the authority of documents, but weighty documents are not substitutes for the richness and denseness of description and explanation grounded in the original data. In all cases, **the researcher must go back to the original data** for confirmation of the descriptions and explanations reported.

Start by writing about the component parts of the research, that is, what is contained in each category. Some of the categories will be saturated and will take some time to describe, while others will contain only a few bibbits and will be described fairly easily. You will probably want to start by describing those files that are saturated. When describing a category, include the main points contained in the file, two or three sample quotations drawn from the bibbits and some comment about the amount of information in the file and degree of saturation. For categories that are unsaturated, the description takes the same form but the wording of the description is more tentative. Both content and process files need to be described.

Bibbits that do not find a home file also need to be described. They are considered unique bits of information which at this time have no known similarities with other bibbits. Sometimes as you write the similarities will become evident. Other times, there simply is no recognizable similarity and the bibbit can simply be described by its uncommon features and the questions it may raise.

b) Beginning to draft the analysis

It is only after thoughtful and complete descriptions that a write-up of the analysis becomes possible. Once you know fully what is located in each category, the possible and probable relationships between categories can be addressed. If you have already done some hurricane thinking to assist with analysis, you will find that you have done some serious rethinking. Relationships are clearer after you have written the categorical descriptions.

Writing about the analysis includes writing about *how* you have done the analysis. Describe and explain as clearly as possible the links between categories and the nature of those links. Also describe the lack of visible links between other categories. Research from the margins is concerned with focussing on what is uncommon among the categories as well as what is common.

The following points may help you with the preparation of a first draft:

1. An outline will help you organize where the various pieces will fit in relation to each other.
2. Get all of the ideas down on paper – do not worry yet about the quality of your writing. The act of writing can spark new ideas; revisions, however extensive, can be done for the final version of the report.
3. You can write blocks of material and reorder it later.
4. Be flexible. Be prepared for sudden turns of events which bring you to new understandings.
5. Ask yourself questions such as:
     is the idea clear?
     are things in the right order, is there a progression?
     is there an illustration I could use from the data?
     is there a schema that would link the data better?
     is there a balance between the description and analysis?
     have I accounted for myself in the write-up?
6. Remember who you are writing the report for. The participants are the first to see it. They should be able to locate their own experience within the document. The final report should be written in such a way as to make it accessible for its expected audience.

With large amounts of data, many interpretations are possible. The more access you have to possible interpretations offered by research participants, and / or other collaborators, the more complete your analysis can be. The pursuit of different interpretations often turns up one or two good alternatives.

No piece of research is perfect. You can acknowledge the shortcomings of your work and point out where the data is too weak to provide direction and where alternative directions are strong. This helps to situate the readers, letting them understand that you are not selling them on the conclusions, but inviting their participation in the analysis of the information and in the construction of the final report. By drafting the report (either in sections or as a complete document) and circulating it to the research participants, researchers can use the comments of research participants to direct the overall report structure, content and agenda for change.

When you are preparing the draft, you may find yourself struggling with some of the following:

1) **The agony of omitting** (Lofland and Lofland, 1984) – Every single bibbit is important but there is no room for it all in the report.

2) The difficulty of guaranteeing equal weight to each bibbit, each saturated category, each link in the analysis — It is not possible to describe each bibbit, each category or each link in equal detail. What you *can* guarantee is that you have attempted to allow all bibbits of information an equal opportunity to become and remain visible within the categories and to describe and explain the data on that basis.

3) The concern about forcing the data analysis — If you choose to include something even though it doesn't fit because you think it is somehow important, simply account for why you are including it. You might write "This doesn't seem to fit but I think it's important and am including it for its individual importance rather than its component importance."

4) The risk of decontextualizing — Because of the mobility of bibbits and categories, it is easy to find that a piece of the data is moving about severed from its context. The careful coding of material will always enable the researcher to relocate the data in the ongoing analysis. Be a disciplined recorder and keep referring to the original copies of the data.

3. Voices in context

There are a number of voices in the draft report: the researcher's, the participants' and the voices of those who have assisted with parts of the research or contributed secondary information. As ideas are explained, the different voices have to be presented in context. Similar to referencing ideas or direct quotes from other people's work, the research report must include a context for each voice. When you, the researcher, are making a point or observation, make sure it is clear that it is the researcher and not any of the other participants. When it is a particular participant, ensure that the brief description meets the guidelines of anonymity but provides enough of a context to situate the information in the participant's reality.

Researchers have the responsibility of reporting on the research in a way that is fair and equitable to participants. This requires a certain personal preparation so that the researcher's voice does not dominate the reporting. Researchers may need time away from the data, away from the analysis and even away from the participants in order to see the particular and the general patterns in the data. There is also the researcher's organizational voice. Researchers are organizers of the participants, collaborators, readers and activists who contribute to the data and to the final reporting on the analysis.

Ensure that the voice of the researcher is present and accounted for in the entire research process, including the final report.

The voices of the researcher and the participants usually differ in two main ways. The first is that the researcher is interested in expressing what a number of people think about a particular experience or topic, rather than concentrating on one individual description. The second is that the researcher is likely to be concerned with discussing how those ideas fit together and how well such patterns explain the topic being researched. While participants may be interested in describing and explaining their experience to the researcher, there may be no corresponding willingness or sense of obligation to become an active seeker of social change. Most participants will not initiate their own research, but will be more aware of the research process and the construction of knowledge after their involvement. Many will influence knowledge creation primarily as participant-collaborators, consumers and interpreters. Others will involve themselves in acting to create change.

Although there can be some movement from description to more theoretical analysis, in the final report the overall reporting should reflect the voices of the participants. Contrasting attitudes among participants are to be presented, within their appropriate context. The researcher's responsibility is to create a forum for presentation of these experiences and ideas rather than seeking the most frequently expressed or the strongest opinions.

You are trying to share with the participants, and later with other readers, how your analysis developed. Therefore, keep to the topic. Explore the ideas that appear to have merit and explain, if you need to, why you do not give the same attention to other ideas in the research. The very act of writing will spark new ideas. Don't let them take over. Rather, incorporate them into your conceptual baggage and include them in the description being formed.

Conclude the draft with an invitation to the participants to make comments about the material. They should be able to see themselves reflected in the research report, within the boundaries of the anonymity that you have guaranteed. Questions addressing specific areas where feedback would be helpful should be considered. For example, you may want their comments on the descriptions, the explanations and the actions identified as important for social change.

We think it essential that some, indeed preferably all, participants see a draft of the report before it is produced in its final form. Comments can be made not only about the draft but about the final destination of the information and the kinds of actions possible to enhance the probability of positive social change. Drafting a research report, knowing that there is room for exploration and elaboration, can make the writing an easier task.

4. Sharing analysis with the research participants

The draft can be shared with research participants in several ways. You could call a small group of participants and / or other collaborators together to discuss the developing analysis and written account. The collective in which the research is being done may want to organize an entirely different group activity so that the researchers experience a freshness in their relationships with each other. This can lead to a new approach to the write-up. You may instead wish to put the whole project away for a week or two and get some distance on the data before you proceed further. Or you may talk the project through with others who are involved in similar areas to get their feedback on your work. In any case, as long as you have a firm grasp of the data, you will not be in any danger of losing your way.

5. Editing for a final report:

The final report is the document which ultimately represents the research. That is, it is the record of the research content, process and analysis as reported by you, the researcher. As the researcher, once you have feedback from the research participants on the draft report, you can begin preparation of the final research report.

At this point, it is important to identify the audience for whom the report is being written. While the content will always be essentially the same, the emphasis on specific points and the way in which they are expressed will be different depending on the target audience. For example, if you are reporting to the general public, your final report will be different than if you report to a collective, a government funding agency or a group of peers who have participated in the research process. The content, style, language and depth need to be tailored to the audience. For some audiences, a short descriptive summary may be what is most needed. For another audience, emphasis on the content may take precedence over any discussion of the method. Write so that you can convey what you know needs to be conveyed to the specific audience(s).

In overall content, this report need not be substantially different from the earlier draft, except where participants have indicated that change is necessary. It should begin with a restatement of the beginnings of the research project and end with a summary section. The summary section provides a description of the knowledge that has been created and a statement on the state of the research at reporting time. Since the research process is an ongoing one, where questions which emerge from one research effort inform subsequent research projects, the final report can suggest how change might occur and lead to new questions for the readers. All in all, it should be a well-presented document that frames the research work appropriately.

ACTING ON WHAT WE KNOW

Researching from the margins is about transforming information into action. Why is transforming knowledge to action so important?

First, any one research project inevitably sparks interest in one or more related projects. There is always a need for new information to fill the gaps, to make visible those people on the margins who have been kept invisible, to debunk the myths and dissolve the misconceptions about those on the margins, to *correct* what is already known and to establish a true tradition of researching where our experience is at the centre of any research process.

Second, researching from the margins will generate new processes for gathering information that incorporate using a dynamic and historical approach where experience in its own context is sought. It recognizes the real life experience, includes those on the margins at the centre of research, and uses a reflexive approach where the researcher is fully accounted for in the process and research addresses issues and actions.

Third, the method of researching from the margins challenges those who engage in androcentric, ethnocentric, sterile and relatively abstracted research. This method challenges the linear approach, the assumed generality of results, the adequacy of terminologies, and the objectivity and identity of the researcher(s). These challenges will have an impact on the monopoly on the production of knowledge, with the result that knowledge created for and by people in the margins will find its place.

1. Getting the word out

There are a variety of ways to get the word out to those who can benefit from the research and / or those who can effect change. In all instances the destination of the information must be carefully considered. The participants and the researcher together must answer the question "Who can benefit from the information?" "What kind of change can be effected with this information?" and "Who might resist the kind of change that we desire?"

The destination of the research information is critical to people in the margins. If there is any question that the information could be used to their detriment, or if it could be used to organize their experience so that it can be further "managed, ordered, regulated and controlled" (Darville, forthcoming), it should not be released. The researcher's responsibility is to take direction about the destination of the research information from the participants and collaborators.

Information should first go to participants, then to others who are involved or willing to work toward change. It is also important to consider how the research information can be released in ways that can contribute to increasing public awareness about, and action on, specific social issues. In all cases, the research must be reported in a way that makes it accessible.

Here are some examples of what has been done with information gathered through the method of researching from the margins:

- Street theatre groups have carried out research in order to write scripts which are then produced and performed as popular education events.
- People have researched the experiences and needs of conference participants in order to generate interest and involve them in the development of the agenda.
- Researchers have used the information gathered from their research to write articles and have them published in community magazines and newspapers.
- Women lobbying for shelters for battered women have set up booths outside shopping malls where they publicized the issue, and carried out their research with the aim of proving the need for a shelter and generating public support for their cause (Mies, 1983).
- People have created leaflets, handbooks, posters, photography shows, slide tape presentations and video tapes full of information to educate people and organize around a specific issue or to lobby the government for specific changes in municipal, provincial and national legislation.
- Cultural workers have done research and used the information as the basis for visual and performing art, music and writing.
- Researchers have organized community research centres to help people acquire the research skills they need to take action on issues that concern them.

2. Moving from research to action

We have been questioning not only **what is researched** and **how research gets done** but also, **why research is done** (McKenna, 1987). Doing research is an equal partner in the following schema:

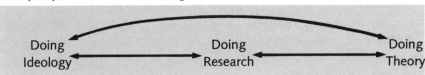

These three are interrelated, each influencing the others directly and indirectly. How we create information informs theory and ideology and is in turn informed by them. When we engage in research from the margins, we need to use methodology in a way that benefits us and, in particular, contributes to social change.

What follows is an example of what happened when students undertook research with little prior discussion with the research coordinators on how ideology or theory may affect their research project.

> In the advanced methods class, students were asked to facilitate an ongoing community research project. The projects were pre-organized[1] and they simply selected the one they liked best. Their task was threefold: a) to facilitate an ongoing project by contributing their skills and abilities to its overall development, b) to keep a reflective journal of their experiences and c) to define "action-research" on the basis of their experience.
>
> Action turned out to be very difficult to define. The student researchers expressed dismay at the strength of pre-organized agendas which guided post-research action and they constantly searched for ways in which the voices of the real participants could be heard. The students also queried whether having one's consciousness raised could be considered action or whether action had to be immediately evident and tangible.
>
> The primary conclusion drawn from the Research Facilitation Project was that the research agenda must be emergent. The motivation for the research had to be based in the researcher's own community and in her experience. All the student researchers had difficulty working so closely with someone else's research agenda when often the experience of the research participants, those with the experience at the root of each project, had so little voice.

Clearly, research and action have to be grounded in the experience of the participants. Often the parameters within which community organizations operate pre-shape what is possible. These projects were not ill-conceived but the lack of attention given to the interrelationship between theory, method and ideology made the projects "undo-able."

---

1. Some examples of projects: a) a student was responsible for organizing community response to disparities in social assistance in the province of Nova Scotia (with Dalhousie Legal Aid Society), b) a student combed through court records prepared by community volunteers to prepare information for a computer analysis of women's experience with the criminal justice system (with the Coverdale Association) and c) a student worked with one of the provincial political parties to gather information from women in the community and prepare policy on sexual harassment.

We believe the research process is an enabling one. From our experience it is clear that as people deliberately engage in this kind of research, as they become creators of knowledge, they become more confident in their ability to "intervene in reality" in a meaningful way. They are less intimidated by traditional research approaches and become better critics of such results.

For example:

> **Lorene**: I think I was able to help the women I interviewed explore a side of themselves that certainly doesn't get as much recognition as it should. After that, I felt I was able to take my own position on topics clearly and strongly right from the beginning. I stopped asking what I should do and instead concentrated on what I knew was needed.

After her research was concluded, Lorene approached other projects with a new confidence in her own abilities as a creator of knowledge. She became a critic of "objectivity" and a strong supporter of experiential research.

Researchers using this approach also describe being much less willing to "give obedience" to outside authority. Here is one woman's reflection on her research:

> I had a partner for 25 years, one whom I chose to leave nearly two years ago because I found myself a victim in a psychologically abusive marriage.... My particular project allowed me to place a new perspective on my own experience. I challenge other women not to be so self-sacrificing in their own life — take time, energy and commitment to ensure your own identity is established and beyond question — above all be self-sufficient. Aim for individual competence more than any other nurturing quality.

The purpose of knowing and of creating knowledge is clear. The creation of knowledge has political ramifications. The method of researching from the margins openly acknowledges and incorporates the personal and political context which underlie investigation, and holds itself accountable for the process of that investigation and for acting with the knowledge created. As one woman expressed it, "the practical application is the bottom line, not identifying the problem." We see other researchers who use methods from the margins as activists in doing research. Our research must matter in the world.

SUMMARY AND CHECKPOINTS

Preparing the draft is the critical step in which the researcher brings together many of the ideas for presentation to various audiences. Since the information has come primarily from the experience of the research participants, it makes sense that the patterns which have emerged from the analysis should stand the test of being shared with the participants. Through this feedback loop in the research process, complications or implications of the research can be considered before the final conclusions are drawn. Feedback from presentation of a draft to the participants can be extraordinarily helpful for refining and accentuating certain parts of the analysis.

The method of researching from the margins incorporates the notion of responsibility; hence the researcher and the participants need to consider what is to be done with the new information.

Checkpoints

- Is my reporting done in a dynamic context?
- Do the voices of the research participants have priority in the research report?
- Is the report usable and readable?
- Does my draft report have the required component parts of a draft report?
- How and when will I share my draft report with research participants?
- What is the final destination of my research report?
- Do I have a plan for action?
- Remember: with knowledge comes the responsibility of acting on that knowledge.

Conclusion

This is a "how-to" book about doing your own research and creating your own knowledge. We use the phrase "doing research" to emphasize that research is a human activity which takes place "in a specific time and place and is engaged in by a specifically located individual, with a specific background, in a specific situation, for a particular series of ends" (Said, 1981:156). How research is done — that is, what questions get asked, of whom, by whom, in what way, how the answers are interpreted — can have far-reaching implications. We can "do research" in a way that helps to maintain or transform current social relations. Our research, like the written word, "can subdue, deceive, pacify and lull, or it can arouse, enlighten, stimulate and awaken" (Bee, 1980:47), depending on the assumptions and processes we employ.

Interpretation underlies the whole process
We reject the assumption that maintaining a separation between politics and knowledge, or theory and practice, is a necessary condition for scholarly activity. Such a claim masks assumptions and ideological principles that often collapse when they are closely examined (Chomsky, 1981; Spender, 1981). This book is based on the assumption that research is a process that involves questions of interpretation and conceptualization; as such, it is a political process.

Researching our experience is part of our action for change

> **Kate**: Without reflection on our actions and experience we will continue to re-invent the wheel, and will remain divided and powerless.

We believe that knowledge construction, if it is to contribute to social change, must be an activity that people can participate in. We have tried to provide a clear "how-to" guide that will enable you to do research beginning with your own experience and research interests. Proceeding from the assumption that all knowledge is socially constructed, we address the political and ethical choices such activity involves, and the ways these choices can be accounted for in the research process.

Doing research from the margins challenges the status quo

The way government policy and laws develop — the kinds of programs that are implemented, the priorities that are set — often hinge on research. We recognize that research is used as a way of regulating the flow of information. Part of the reason for keeping research tools cloaked in mystery is that this enables people who do have access to them to claim special skill and expertise, to claim that what they know **is** objective, that it is the way knowledge must be constructed, and that there are no other options.

We care about the accessibility of research skills because we believe that people should have the opportunity to inform themselves, to participate in discussion and policy formation and advance their interests through political action. Demystifying research skills challenges current social relations in which expertise remains a source of power for a few rather than a resource available to all. Doing research allows us to begin to rename our experience, and thus participate in creating knowledge we can use.

The process is emergent

The method we describe here is not cast in stone. Because people have different experiences, they have different research needs. Part of what it means to do research from the margins is that as you use the method you will contribute to how the method develops. We think of research from the margins as method in process: it is continually unfolding.

Doing research can be empowering and fun.

There is power in being able to tell your story and hearing others tell theirs. Sharing experiences triggers some life, some anger, some need to create change. The research process we describe is exciting and creative. Because it is rooted in your experience and your research needs, you will find youself living your research. The most important thing you can do now is get started.

Bibliography

Babbie, Earl. 1985. *The Practice of Social Research.* Belmont, Calif.:
  Wadsworth Publishing Company.

Bee, Barbara. 1980. "The Politics of Literacy." In R. Mackie, ed., *Literacy
  and Revolution.* London: Pluto Press.

Blier, Ruth. 1984. *Science and Gender.* Oxford: Pergamon Press.

Bowles, Gloria, and Renata Duelli Klein, eds. 1983. *Theories of Women's
  Studies.* London: Routledge & Kegan Paul.

Burt, Sandra, Lorraine Code, and Lindsey Dorney, eds. 1988. *Changing
  Patterns: Women in Canada.* Toronto: McClelland and Stewart.

Carney, T.F. 1983. *Qualitative Methods in Communication Studies: A New
  Paradigm Research Manual.* Windsor: Department of Communication
  Studies, The University of Windsor.

Chadwick, Bruce A., Howard A. Bahr, and Stan L. Albrecht. 1984. *Social
  Science Research Methods.* Englewood Cliffs, N.J.: Prentice-Hall.

Chomsky, Noam. 1981. *Radical Priorities.* Montreal: Black Rose Books.

Code, Lorraine, Sheila Mullett, and Christine Overall, eds. 1988. *Feminist
  Perspectives: Philosophical Essays on Methods and Morals.* Toronto:
  University of Toronto Press.

Connell, R.W., D.J. Ashenden, S. Kessler, and G.W. Dowsett. 1982. *Making
  The Difference.* Sydney: George Allen & Unwin.

Currie, Andrea. 1988. *Funding Guidelines for Nova Scotia Women's
  Groups.* Halifax, Canada: Project Report for the Canadian Congress for
  Learning Opportunities for Women.

Darville, Richard. "The Language of Experience and the Literacy of Power."
  In J. Draper and M. Taylor, eds., *Adult Basic Education: A Field of
  Practice.* Culture Concepts Inc., forthcoming.

Denzin, Norman K. 1970. *The Research Act: a Theoretical Introduction to Sociological Methods.* Chicago: Aldine Publishing Company.

Devor, Holly. 1988. "Female to Male Transexuals" (working title). Dissertation in progress, Simon Fraser University.

Dooley, David. 1984. *Social Research Methods.* Englewood Cliffs, N.J.: Prentice-Hall.

Eichler, Margrit and Jeanne Lapointe. 1985. *On The Treatment of the Sexes in Research.* Ottawa: Social Sciences and Humanities Research Council.

Erickson, Erik H. 1963. *Childhood and Society.* 2nd ed. New York: Norton Publishing Company.

Finson, Shelley Davis. 1985. "On the Other Side of Silence: Patriarchy, Consciousness and Silence – Some Women's Experience of Theological Education." D.Min. thesis. Boston University, Boston.

Freire, Paulo. 1985. *The Politics of Education.* South Hadley, Mass.: Bergin and Garvey Publishers.

George, Susan. 1976. *How the Other Half Dies.* New York: Penguin Books.

Glaser, Barney G. and Anselm Strauss. 1967. *The Discovery of Grounded Theory: Strategies for Qualitative Research.* Chicago: Aldine Press.

Glassner, B. and J. Corzine. 1982. "Library Research as Fieldwork: A Strategy for Qualitative Analysis." *Sociology and Social Research,* 66(2): 305-319.

Griffin, Susan. 1982. "The Way of All Ideology." *Signs,* 7(3):641-60.

Hanmer, Jalna and Sheila Saunders. 1984. *Well-Founded Fear: a community study of violence to women.* London: Hutchinson.

Harding, Sandra, ed. 1987. *Feminism and Methodology.* Bloomington: Open University Press / Indiana University Press.

Harman, Lesley D. 1989. *When A Hostel Becomes A Home: The Experience of Women.* Toronto: Garamond.

hooks, bell. 1984. *Feminist Theory: from margin to centre.* Boston: South End Press.

Jackson, Winston. 1988. *Research Methods: Rules for Survey Design and Analysis.* Scarborough, Canada: Prentice-Hall Inc.

Johnson, John M. 1975. *Doing Field Research.* New York: The Free Press.

Kirby, Sandra L. 1980. "Preferred Coaching Styles Among Novice and Elite Rowers, Canoers and Kayakers." M.A. thesis. McGill University, Montreal.

Kirby, Sandra L. 1982. "Women in Rowing." *CATCH* (Spring / Summer).

Kirby, Sandra L. 1986. *High Performance Female Athlete Retirement.* Ph.D. dissertation, University of Alberta, Edmonton.

Kirby, Sandra L. and K. McKenna. 1988. "Action Research in Women's Studies: a Dialogue Between Two Feminists." Paper presented at the

Canadian Women's Studies Association annual meeting, Windsor, June.

Krieger, Susan. 1983. *The Mirror Dance: Identity in a Women's Community.* Philadelphia: Temple University Press.

LeRougetel, Amanda. 1987. "The Women's Beat: Anne Rauhala." Unpublished paper, School of Journalism, King's University, Halifax.

The Living Webster Encyclopedic Dictionary. 1974. Chicago: The English Language Institute of America.

Lofland, John and Lyn Lofland. 1984. *Analyzing Social Settings,* (2nd Ed.). Belmont, Calif.: Wadsworth Publishing Company.

Lorde, Audre. 1984. *Sister Outsider.* New York: The Crossing Press.

Marshall, Doris. 1987. *Silver Threads: Critical Reflections on Growing Old.* Toronto: Between The Lines.

Matthews, Sarah. 1978. *The Social World Of Old Women.* Beverly Hills, Calif.: Sage Publications.

McKenna, Kate. 1987. "Feminist Theory in Sociology." Unpublished research paper, Mount Saint Vincent University, Halifax.

McKenna, Rebecca. 1988. Personal interview, May.

Mies, Maria. 1983. "Towards a methodology for feminist research." In G. Bowles and R. Duelli Klein, eds., *Theories of Women's Studies.* London: Routledge & Kegan Paul.

Mies, Maria. 1986. *Patriarchy and Accumulation on a World Scale.* London: Zed Books Ltd.

Miller, Brian. 1983. "Identity Conflict and Resolution: A Social Psychological Model of Gay Familymen's Adaptations." Ph.D. dissertation, University of Alberta, Edmonton.

Mishler, Elliot G. 1984. *The Discourse of Medicine: Dialectics of Medical Interviews.* Norwood, N.J.: Ablex Publishing Company.

Morgan, Gareth. 1983. *Beyond Method.* Beverly Hills, Calif.: Sage Publications.

Moyer, Bill. 1986. "The Movement Action Plan." *The Dandelion,* Fall.

Ng, Roxana. 1987. Personal communication, June.

Ng, Roxana. 1988. *The Politics of Community Services: Immigrant Women, Class and State.* Toronto: Garamond Press.

Oakley, Ann. 1981. *Subject Women.* New York: Pantheon Books.

Pettigrew, Joyce. 1981. "Reminiscences of Fieldwork among the Sikhs." In H. Roberts, ed., *Doing Feminist Research.* London: Routledge & Kegan Paul.

"The Politics of Information." *IDEAS.* 1983. Toronto: C.B.C. Radio, May.

Prus, R. and S. Irini. 1980. *Hookers, Rounders and Desk Clerks: The Social Organization of a Hotel Community.* Toronto: Gage Publishing Company.

Purcell, Neil. 1987. "A Seven Day Simulation of a Severe Bilateral Hearing Impairment: A Qualitative Analysis." M.Ed. thesis. Université de Moncton, Moncton.

Reinharz, Shulamit. 1983. "Experimental Analysis: A Contribution to Feminist Analysis." In G. Bowles, and R. Duelli Klein, eds., *Theories of Women's Studies.* London: Routledge & Kegan Paul.

Rich, Adrienne. 1979. *On Lies, Secrets and Silence.* New York: W.W. Norton.

Richlin-Klonsky, J. and E. Strenski, eds. 1986. *A Guide to Writing Sociology Papers.* New York: St. Martin's Press.

Roberts, Helen. 1981. *Doing Feminist Research.* London: Routledge & Kegan Paul.

Said, Edward W. 1981. *Covering Islam: How the Media and the Experts Determine How We See the Rest of the World.* New York: Pantheon Books.

Sharpe, Errol. 1988. Personal communication, July.

Sherwood, H.C. 1969. *The Journalistic Interview.* New York: Harper and Row.

Smith, Dorothy. 1979. "A sociology for women." In Julia Sherman, and Evelyn T. Beck, eds., *The Prism of Sex: Essays in Sociology of Knowledge.* Madison: University of Wisconsin Press.

Smith, Dorothy. 1984. "Textually mediated social organization." *International Social Science Journal,* 36(1):59-75.

Smith, Dorothy. 1987. *The Everyday World as Problematic.* Toronto: University of Toronto Press.

Spender, Dale. 1981. *Men's Studies Modified.* Oxford: Pergamon Press.

Stanley, Liz and Sue Wise. 1983. *Breaking Out: Feminist Consciousness and Feminist Research.* London: Routledge & Kegan Paul.

Webb, E.J., D.T. Campbell, R.D. Schwartz, and L. Sechrest. 1966. *Unobtrusive Measures: Nonreactive Research in the Social Sciences.* Chicago: Rand McNally.

Weinstein, Gail. 1984. "Literacy and Second Language Acquisition: Issues and Perspectives." *TESOL Quarterly,* 18(3):471-84.

Westergaard, John and Henrietta Resler. 1975. *Class in a Capitalist Society: A Study of Contemporary Britain.* New York: Basic Books.

Wheeler, Charlene E. and Peggy Chinn. 1984. *Peace and Power: A Handbook of Feminist Process.* Buffalo, NY: Margaretdaughters Inc.

Williams, Raymond. 1976. *Key Words. A Vocabulary of Culture and Society.* London: Croom Helm.

APPENDIX A
DESCRIPTION OF RESEARCH PROJECTS

Andrea Currie: When Sandi mentioned that "a problem," or "tensions" having to do with a problem, were clues we could use to lead us to a research question, I knew immediately that I had to focus on relationships. Not only does my life not seem to fit into the patterns of patriarchal culture, but I cannot even find words that adequately express my reality. I was interested in critically examining the dynamic between the language available to us and the meanings we try to express and explore.

Anne MacIntyre: I selected this topic from a deep political need to understand how a person who has spent most of her life following the rules of a "just" society can be so badly burned, and also in some small way perhaps to share my limited knowledge of this subject as a warning to other women. I had a partner for twenty-five years, one who I chose to leave two years ago, and because I still "favor the place where the knife went in," it was important for me to understand why it happened and by doing so, perhaps let go. And so my topic evolved: "How and under what conditions do women come to a decision to leave a marriage?: from the perspective of an abused wife."

Brenda Thompson: I decided to do my research on "welfare" mothers because I am a "welfare" mother. I also wanted to do this research because of the whole experience I have gone through and continue to encounter since I stood up for myself and other Nova Scotians when I refused to be treated as a lower human being simply because I am poor.

Brenda White: I decided that I wanted to do something about me and working. I am in the process of changing my profession but couldn't find any research that really spoke to me about what I am experiencing and why. I wanted to find a way of researching that would address these issues.

Catherine Butler: Sandi said: "Pick something you want to know more about that is grounded in your experience." Well when the topic is incest, and your reason for choosing the topic is because it is your own experience, it is very difficult to pinpoint the exact time when you chose it as a research topic. By the time the course came along I was overripe. I not only wanted to do it, I needed to do it. I was longing for the structure this class could give me to enable me to deal with this topic.

All of these women participated in Feminist Methods courses taught at Mount St. Vincent University in Halifax between 1986 and 1988. Since the researchers are referred to by their first names throughout the book, the alphabetical arrangement is also done by first name.

Colleen Purcell: I worked on a topic that I decided not to name in class. It involved chronicalling experiences of a personal nature and I was able to work with the process in a collaborative way with other researchers. It was very helpful that I was still able to participate fully in class and the others gave me the room I needed to gather information from diaries and analyze the content. My greatest problem throughout was that, as a mother of four children, I was always thinking about the topic and seldom had the time to record my reflections on the material. I devised creative ways of recording information so that ideas would not slip by.

Florence Chaytor: I wanted to know whether other mature women experienced their decision to return to university as I did. I was interested in the process that brought this decision about, the steps involved and their reaction to that experience. My research question was "What motivates a woman in mid-life to return to university?"

Heather Dunbar: I had initially begun with an altogether different topic which I reconsidered after my second interview left me with very negative feelings about the subject matter. At this point I really didn't know what I wanted to find out; I only knew what I wanted to do, and who I wanted to interview. I had decided I wanted to interview three women who held positions in the province of Nova Scotia that no female had held before.

Judie MacDougall: I chose to research "speaking from the edge" because of my experience trying to communicate in two very different social worlds, one academic and feminist and the other non-academic and non-feminist. I understood at the start that my research project would not change the lives of many people but I thought it would have some impact on my life and the lives of those around me.

Kate McKenna: My question was formulated from a problem I encountered during a course on contemporary sociological theory when I suggested presenting feminist theory as a topic. In response it was suggested that I present feminism as a critique, since feminists had made many important critiques of sociology. This baffled me. If feminists were making admittedly important critiques these must be based on certain theoretical asssumptions which could be identified. Was it that these assumptions did not fall inside the framework of what is considered sociological? Or did it reveal something about the interests of those who control what enters the discourse? Not satisfied with presenting feminism merely as a critique of any discipline, I began reading to try to discover criteria for what is regarded as "legitimate" sociological theory.

At this same time I was also trying to identify a research topic for Sandi's course. I began to get excited when I considered the possibility of taking these questions about feminist theory in sociology as the focus for my research project. The project, initially one of three months' duration, soon extended into eleven months of research, reflection and writing.

Lorene Dobbie: I was already aware of the content of the course and what it entailed because I had spoken with women who took it the previous year. So I came to the class knowing I wanted / needed to explore spirituality and, in particular, feminist spirituality. My initial questions involved asking "What does spirituality mean for other women?" and "Can there be a liberating feminist spirituality?"

Robbie McGinn: The idea for my research emerged from a feeling of anger. I was a member of an International Women's Day committee. We were an ad hoc committee of eight women and our intention was to organize events at Mount St. Vincent University to celebrate I.W.D. In the process we had incurred the disapproval of the Student Council by including, among other events, a women's only pub night. Although at the time I chose my research focus we had not yet been forbidden to hold the event, the fact that it was considered questionable angered all of us. My research focussed on chronicalling these events.

Sarah Billard: I couldn't put it off any longer, I *had* to do this topic. I kept coming up with reasons why I *should not,* and tried to begin researching a number of other topics. However, my writing kept telling me that I could not afford to use this opportunity to research any topic but lesbianism. Finally, through writing my conceptual baggage, I found my question: "Why are explanations of lesbianism necessary and for whom?"

Tarel Quandt: My research question arose from the struggle I was having with the feeling that I did not fit in with my age group. Traditionally, once a female reaches her late teens, early twenties, she is expected to become engaged and marry. I was interested in discovering whether young women were aware of this expectation and, if so, how they reacted to it.

APPENDIX B
ANNOTATED BIBLIOGRAPHY

Bowles, Gloria and Renate Duelli Klein, eds. 1983. *Theories of Women's Studies.* London: Routledge & Kegan Paul.

The book contains an excellent discussion of the assumptions and aims of Women's Studies as a discipline and the emerging methodologies appropriate to it. It is full of interesting innovations and offers important critiques of male stream method.

Code, Lorraine, Sheila Mullett and Christine Overall, eds. 1988. *Feminist Perspectives: Philosophical Essays on Method and Morals.* Toronto: University of Toronto Press.

This is a collection of articles that illustrate how the doing of philosophy changes when the philosopher is feminist. It addresses the essential ambivalence of an individual shaped by philosophical traditions yet needing to change some of those traditions.

Hanmer, Jalna and Sheila Saunders. 1984. *Well-Founded Fear: A community study of violence to women.* London: Hutchinson.

"The main aim of this book is to encourage women's groups to undertake their own research into violence to women" (p. 11). The book uses the description of one specific community research project to flush out some of the methodological and ethical issues involved in the research process. It is both a "how-to" manual and an exposé of the cycle of violence. The book is written in clear and direct language. Illustrations, easy-to-read tables, the questionnaire from the study and a chart that pulls together the analysis all add to the accessibility of their work. It shows that good research can be done by non-academics with little or no funding.

Harding, Sandra, ed. 1987. *Feminism and Methodology.* Bloomington: Open University Press / Indiana University Press.

Harding explores new ways to use familiar research methods, new questions to ask and new ways of asking them. Her critique of the scientific method is a valuable one. The essays included in this book are authored by some of the best known women in a number of disciplines: Joan Kelly-Gadol, Carolyn Wood Sherif, Carol Gilligan, Dorothy E. Smith, Catharine MacKinnon and Nancy Hartsock. In particular, this work examines social change and social responsibility from the perspective of the social relations between men and women.

Krieger, Susan. 1983. *The Mirror Dance: Identity in a Women's Community*. Philadelphia: Temple University Press.

This is the research account of a participant observation of a lesbian community in the late 1970's in the U.S.A. which reads like a novel. Krieger makes several methodologically important points about the use of the language from the community, the role of the researcher in the community, the distance needed from the community in order to write and the fine line between fiction and realistic reporting. In her reporting she sought to "create a sense of the whole" (p.xvi) and she asks how this is different from a science which forms a "probable reflection" of how life is lived.

Lofland, John, and Lyn H. Lofland. 1984. *Analyzing Social Settings,* (2nd ed.). Belmont, Calif.: Wadsworth Publishing Company.

As qualitative methods became ever more popular, Lofland and Lofland recognized the need for a comprehensive step-by-step guide for researchers using qualitative observation and analysis. It is well thought out, well organized and an essential part of any researcher's library.

MacLean, Eleanor. 1981. *Between the Lines: How to Detect Bias and Propaganda in the News and Everyday Life*. Montreal: Black Rose Books.

Between the Lines is an exploration of ways to "de-code" the media. With special reference to how events in the "Third World" are reported, it outlines methods of analysis, providing sections on clear thinking, on how news is constructed and how to detect bias. "The book's main purpose is to initiate a *process of questioning and investigation.*"

Marshall, Doris. 1987. *Silver Threads: Critical Reflections on Growing Old*. Toronto: Between the Lines.

This is a delightful account of one woman's struggle to make change. Marshall uses her life experience as the common thread and builds a critique of bureaucratic structures and the lack of research opportunities in the field of aging. She writes the book in the hope that "*in so doing, it will be possible to see, through the prism of my lifetime, how the way we live our lives has changed over the years, and what must be done if old people are, in fact, to see themselves and be seen as persons of worth and value*" (p. 14).

Matthews, Sarah H. 1979. *The Social World of Old Women: Management of Self-Identity*. Beverly Hills, Calif.: Sage Publications.

Matthews presents a straightforward account of her research process beginning with the identification of the problem and ending with the solution to
the research question. At the beginning, she did not know what "old" was
and, through surveys, interviews and recorded conversations, she was able
to construct for the reader a description of what "old" meant to old women.
The voices of the women are central to the account.

Ng, Roxàna. 1988. *The Politics of Community Services: Immigrant Women,
    Class and State.* Toronto: Garamond Press.

The Politics of Community Services is a useful resource both as an example
of how one researcher used participant observation, documentary analysis
and interviews to analyze the internal transformation of a community
employment agency, and because the issue which it addresses, the effects of
state funding on community groups, raises important questions for all
researchers.

Dian Marino. 1981. *Drawing From Action For Action: drawing and
    discussion as a popular research tool.* PRG Working Paper #6. Toronto:
    Participatory Research Group.

A discussion of how drawing can be used as a resource for collective inquiry.

Progressive Literacy Group, 1986. *Writing on Our Side.* Box 66147 Station F,
    Vancouver.

Writing on Our Side was written by people who are active in progressive literacy work. It is a clear and very readable discussion about how to write in
language that makes what you have to say accessible to as many people as
possible. It is a useful guide for researchers who are concerned about getting
the word out.

Roberts, Helen, ed. 1981. *Doing Feminist Research.* London: Routledge &
    Kegan Paul.

This collection of papers presents an account of sociological work which has
been influenced by feminism or feminist critiques. Beginning from the
assumption that problems encountered in personal research are sociologi-
cally important, and offering important insights which are not usually shared
in method texts, the book "examines some of the theoretical, practical,
methodological and ethical issues raised by the recognition that social
processes are affected by sexual as well as class divisions" (Roberts, 1981:1).

Stanley, Liz and Sue Wise. 1983. *Breaking Out: Feminist Consciousness and Feminist Research.* London: Routledge & Kegan Paul.

The main theme of this book is that of doing research from feeling and experience. It highlights the principle of claiming one's personal position in the construction of knowledge: "It doesn't feel right to us, and this feeling occurs because what they say is belied by our experience" (p. 177). Research is a process and the researcher is the medium for this process. Stanley and Wise encourage the readers to break out of objectivity, rationality and experiment and find subjectivity, emotionality and experience.

Smith, Dorothy. 1987. *The Everyday World as Problematic.* Toronto: University of Toronto Press.

The Everyday World as Problematic is a collection of essays which document the development of Dorothy Smith's analytic thinking. The papers "address the problem of a sociology written from the standpoint of men located in the relations of ruling our societies. They propose and formulate a sociology for the standpoint of women and follow through its implications for research" (Smith, 1987:1).

Index

Access to data sites 10, 16, 24, 27, 33, 43, 60, 75, 93, 98, 101-04, 114, 117-9, 160, 164, 170, 178, 180

Andrea 24, 60-1, 124, 171, 175

Anne 67, 130, 173, 175

Anonymity 100, 112, 117-8, 132, 161-2

Appropriateness 102-3, 114

Assumptions 21, 26, 32-3, 42, 51-3, 64-5, 94, 130, 142, 151, 169, 176, 178

Babbie, Earl 171

Bee, Barbara 16, 169, 171

Being honourable 21, 31, 55, 78, 122

Bias 44, 63, 179

Bibbits 129, 135-41, 144-6, 148-9, 152, 154, 159, 161

Blier, Ruth 171

Brenda T. 23, 79, 100, 118, 175

Brenda W. 126, 141,147-8,150

Burt, Sandra 171

Carney, T.F. 128, 150, 171

Categories 11, 37, 60, 128-9, 137-9, 141-50, 152, 154, 159, 161

Catherine 24, 47, 50, 83, 91, 92, 121, 144, 175

Celebrating 123

Chadwick, Bruce 171

Chomsky, Noam 23, 27, 33, 164, 171

Code 37, 139

Code, Lorraine 171, 178

Coding 24, 110, 129, 132, 135, 136, 138-9, 140-1, 145, 154, 161

Collaborators 27, 31, 35-6, 70-1, 73, 104, 107, 112, 118, 120, 129, 150, 160-4

Colleen 73, 78, 125, 144, 176

Communication 32, 74, 78-9, 98-101, 171, 173-4

Community 6, 18, 28, 45, 48, 55, 69, 70-1, 78, 84, 91, 108, 120, 151, 165, 166, 172-3, 178-80

Conceptual baggage 8-9, 21, 32, 37, 44, 47, 49-54, 58, 60-2, 66, 72, 76, 85-88, 97, 102, 107-8, 119, 131, 133, 138, 141, 144-5, 150, 156-7, 162, 169, 177

Connell, R.W. 26, 171

Context 7, 8, 11, 15-6, 21-23, 28-9, 33-4, 42, 47, 52-3, 55, 68, 75, 77, 81-2, 84, 119, 124-5, 129, 130, 133, 135-7, 141, 155, 161-2, 164, 167-8

Creators 10, 44, 54, 95, 167

Currie, Andrea 171, 175

Darville, Richard 16, 18, 164, 171

Denzin, Norman 66, 74, 81, 83, 84, 85, 172

Destination 26, 71, 112, 150, 162, 164, 168

Devor, Holly 99, 172

Dooley, David 79, 172

Dorney, Lindsey 171

Doublethink / Doublespeak 24, 31, 33, 64

Eichler, Margrit 85, 172

Emergent 27, 32, 41, 73, 81, 94, 143, 145, 152, 159, 166, 170

Equality 7, 17, 26-7, 33, 67, 104

Erickson, Erik 42, 172

Ethics 8, 67, 102, 104, 112, 114, 143

Facts 23, 24, 25, 28, 34, 129

Feminist 5, 15, 19, 31, 46, 51, 65, 72, 106, 108, 119, 120, 142, 149, 151-2, 171-8, 180-1
Field Notes 21, 32, 55-6, 58-9, 67, 79, 81, 89, 103, 112-13, 124-6, 133, 135-7, 144, 150, 171, 172-3, 179
Files 11, 109, 124, 129, 131-5, 138-42, 144-6, 149, 152, 154, 156-9
Finson, Shelley Davis 32, 42, 68, 99, 129, 172
Florence 176
Focussing 9, 18, 33, 44, 46, 49, 52-3, 55, 60-1, 98, 159
Freire, Paulo 28, 34, 58, 129, 172
George, Susan 27, 171, 172
Getting the word out 164
Glaser, Barney 20, 81, 85, 93, 129, 135, 137-8, 172
Glassner, B. 57, 172
Griffin, Susan 31, 172
Grounded
 in data 149, 158-9
 in experience 61, 64, 110, 136, 166, 175
 theory 20, 110, 129, 137, 172
Hanmer, Jalna 69, 71, 75, 172, 178
Harding, Sandra 172, 178
Heather 90, 91, 116, 176
Hermeneutic 32, 42, 136
Hierarchy 32, 53
hooks, bell 5, 65, 172
Hurricane Thinking 129, 146-8, 150, 152, 154, 158-9
Identity 11, 48, 50, 70, 87, 98, 101, 116-7, 119, 131-2, 164, 167, 173, 179
Ideology 24, 33, 63, 165-6, 172
Instinct 31, 51, 97, 107, 121
Intensive Interviews 68, 69, 74
Interpretation 23-5, 32-3, 42, 83-4, 86, 108, 115, 124, 148, 150, 156, 160, 169
Intersubjectivity 28, 34, 99, 129, 130
Jackson, Winston 172
Johnson, John 85, 131, 172
Judie 106, 176
Kate 3, 5, 18, 36, 64, 67, 108, 119, 142, 152, 169, 173, 176
Kirby, Sandra L. 3, 19, 42-3, 172
Klein, Duelli 78, 171, 173-4, 178
Knowledge
 acting on 18, 168
 construction of 170, 181
 creation of 7, 10, 16-7, 10, 21-2,

24-5, 27, 29, 32, 31 33, 52, 54, 94, 97, 110, 156, 167-9
 definition of 25-6, 169
 power 15, 23, 65
 production of 15, 28, 33, 63, 95, 102, 164
 social 65, 103
Krieger, Susan 48, 78, 173, 179
Layering 52, 53, 59, 102, 109, 141, 156
Legitimate 21, 23, 27, 33, 63, 104, 176
LeRougetel, Amanda 5, 173
Library Tour 9, 54-60, 62, 82, 93, 107, 125, 172, 179
Life history (histories) 10, 65, 76, 81-6, 92-2, 107, 113, 119, 125, 143, 151
Literacy 15, 16, 18, 171, 174, 180
Literature review 55, 60, 102, 123, 133
Lofland and Lofland 46, 66, 74, 85, 102-5, 114, 118, 150, 160, 173, 179
Lorde, Audre 65, 173
Lorene 46, 70, 98, 99, 100, 116, 141-2, 167, 177
Marshall, Doris 48, 173, 179
Matthews, Sarah 173, 179-80
McKenna 3, 165, 172-3, 176
Mies, Maria 15, 25, 72, 165, 173
Miller, Brian 48, 99, 173
Mishler, Elliot 108, 115, 173
Morgan, Garreth 25-6, 173
Moyer, Bill 25, 173
Ng, Roxana 32, 71, 173, 180
Oakley, Ann 66-7, 173
Oppression 32, 48
Permission 69, 84, 87, 89, 92-3, 98, 112-4, 116-9
Pettigrew, Joyce 103, 173
Planning 41, 44, 54, 63, 95, 97, 99, 101, 103, 105, 107, 109, 110-11, 128, 155-7
Politics 15, 46, 71, 86, 169, 171-3, 180
Positivism 34
Power 15, 17, 19, 23, 26-8, 32-5, 41, 53, 65, 67, 84, 93, 103, 105, 136, 140, 169, 170-1, 174
Praxis 25, 34, 142, 151, 156
Preparation 5, 60, 75, 115, 117, 135, 160-1, 163
Property 135, 139

Prus, Robert 78, 173
Purcell, Neil 5, 174, 176
Rage 5, 18, 29, 35, 65, 72, 75, 83,
    101, 104, 110, 126, 178, 181
Refocus 37, 60, 62
Reinharz, Shulamit 78, 156, 174
Reliability 35
Report 11, 21, 26, 35, 37, 41, 43, 74,
    77-8, 80, 83, 85, 93, 96, 99, 104,
    108, 112, 115, 119, 125, 133, 146,
    155-64, 168, 171, 179
Rich, Adrienne 15, 18, 171, 174
Richlin-Klonsky, J. 174
Robbie 51, 77, 84, 98, 120, 148-9,
    177
Roberts, Helen 47, 85, 103, 173, 174,
    180
Said, Edward 23, 32, 169, 174
Sarah 46, 61, 70, 72, 98, 116, 173,
    177, 179
Satellite 135, 146, 149, 152
Saturation 123, 138, 144, 146, 159
Sexism 77
Sharpe, Errol 5, 174
Sherwood, H.C. 174

Smith, Dorothy 5, 18, 24, 26, 28, 33,
    35, 52, 64, 114, 174, 178, 181
Spender, Dale 28, 95, 169, 174
Stanley, Liz 17, 34, 48-9, 174, 181
Strauss, Anselm 20, 81, 85, 93, 129,
    135, 137-8, 172
Survey 10, 19, 21, 65, 73-6, 81, 85-6,
    88, 89, 92, 99, 102, 107-8, 113-7,
    119, 120-1, 123, 125, 133-4, 154,
    157, 172, 180
Tarel 51, 61, 99, 108, 115, 141, 147,
    177
Theory 5, 31, 32, 36, 63, 65, 81,
    119-20, 129, 135, 137-8, 142-3,
    151-2, 165-6, 169, 172-3, 176-7
Thought cloth 36, 57, 59, 62, 154
Truth 7, 15, 24, 33
Validity 36
Webb, E.J. 174
Weinstein, Gail 16, 174
Westergaard, John 34, 174
Wheeler, Charlene 174
Williams, Raymond 131, 174
Wise, Sue 17, 34, 48-9, 174, 181